ZEN Animals

A Complete Guide to Master Wild Animals Drawing in Zen Doodle

by Daniele Ling

Table of contents

Disclaimer

While all attempts have been made to verify the information provided in this book, the author does assume any responsibility for errors, omissions, or contrary interpretations of the subject matter contained within. **The information provided in this book is for educational and entertainment purposes only. The reader is responsible for his or her own actions and the author does not accept any responsibilities for any liabilities or damages, real or perceived, resulting from the use of this information.**

The trademarks that are used are without any consent, and the publication of the trademark is without permission or backing by the trademark owner. All trademarks and brands within this book are for clarifying purposes only and are the owned by the owners themselves, not affiliated with this document.

Introduction

Hello there! Welcome to this drawing course. We hope that you can find this workbook useful for your artistic needs; better yet, we assure you that we will meet your expectations. In the following six chapters, we will help you grasp the basics of the ZEN style of sketches.

"ZEN Animals - A Complete Guide to Master Wild Animals Drawing in Zendoodle" is going to be an entertaining experience for you. The doodles here shown will help you pass time by, relax, and brush up on this art form; certainly it will prove to be quite the nice reading experience for you, the reader.

We know that we are being repetitive at this, although it bears on being told again and again, you are going to get the knack of this in record time. As we are being insistent, we should also mention yet again how much this hobby doubles as manner of alleviation. Striking lines or fiddling some curves, this will be an amazing time waster.

This book provides such easy exercises that you will be mastering ZEN doodle quite easily. Take paper and markers; practice lots and lots. Remember: it does not matter how difficult a picture looks, it always can be deconstructed to be basic shapes. Let's just begin.

Drawing level 1: Look! Here comes the circus elephant

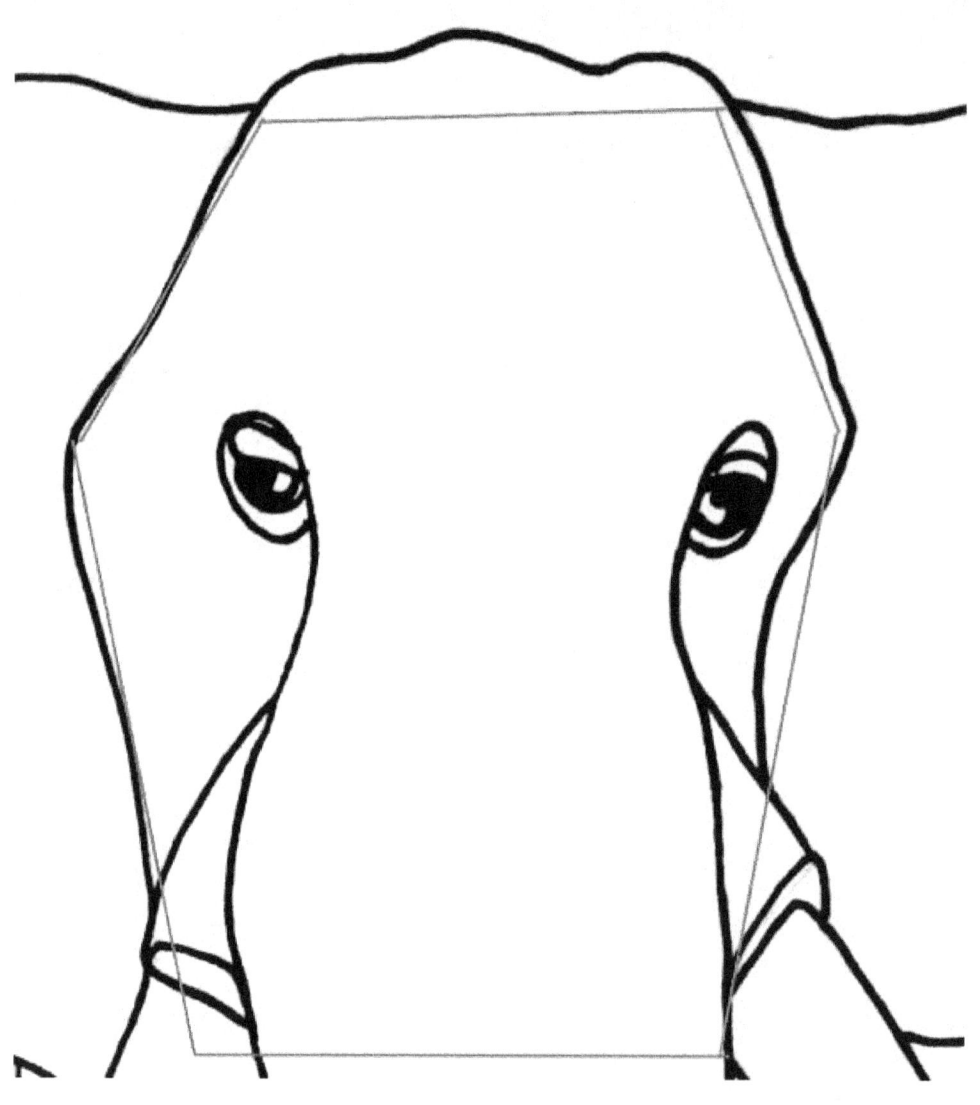

Step one: The first thing you will notice looking the drawing right up is that the elephant face is inside some sort of hexagon. So to begin this, we will draw something with a similar shape of a hexagon; do not worry about not making it perfect-it is not supposed to be-.

Step two: Now look to the sides of the trump, from where the tusks comes; betting that you noticed how they are triangle shaped. Draw them. One at each side of the trump.

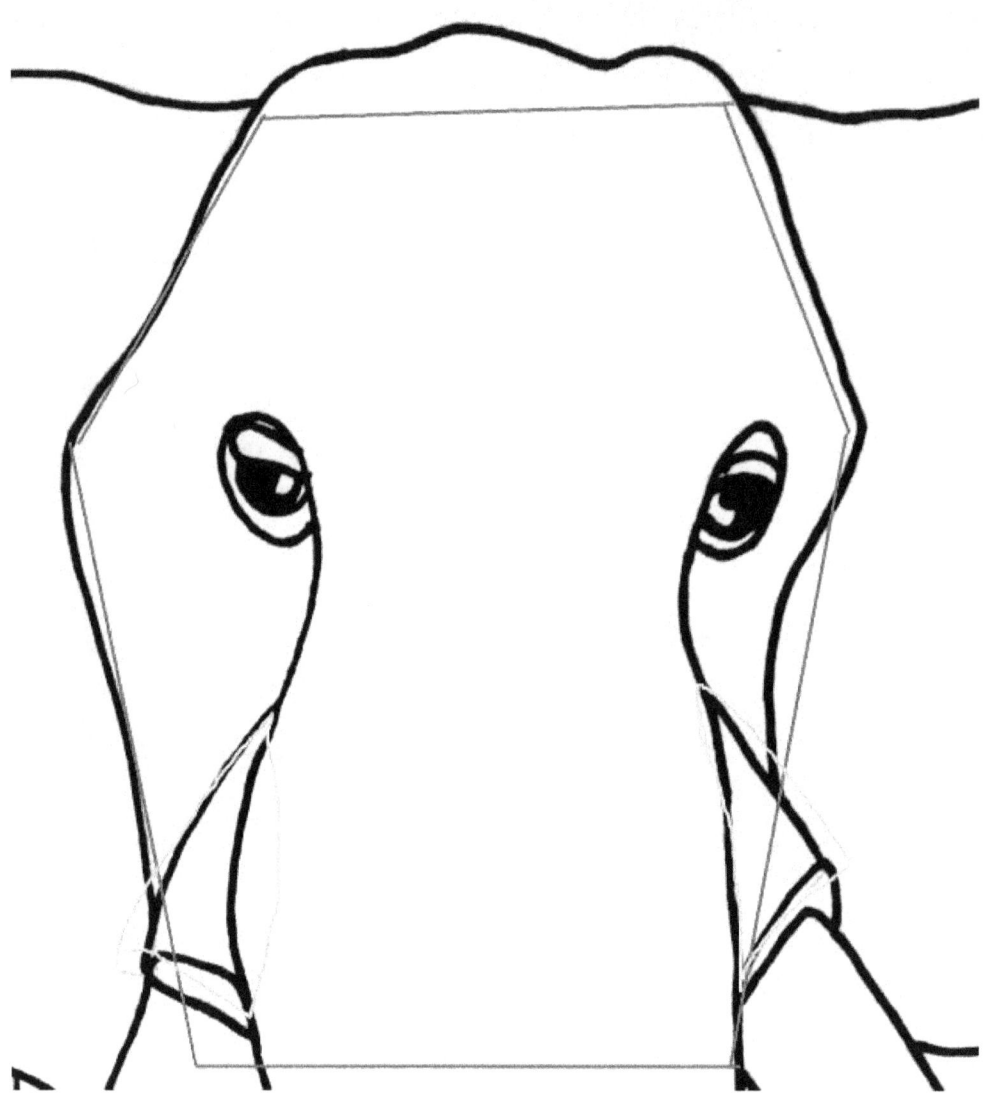

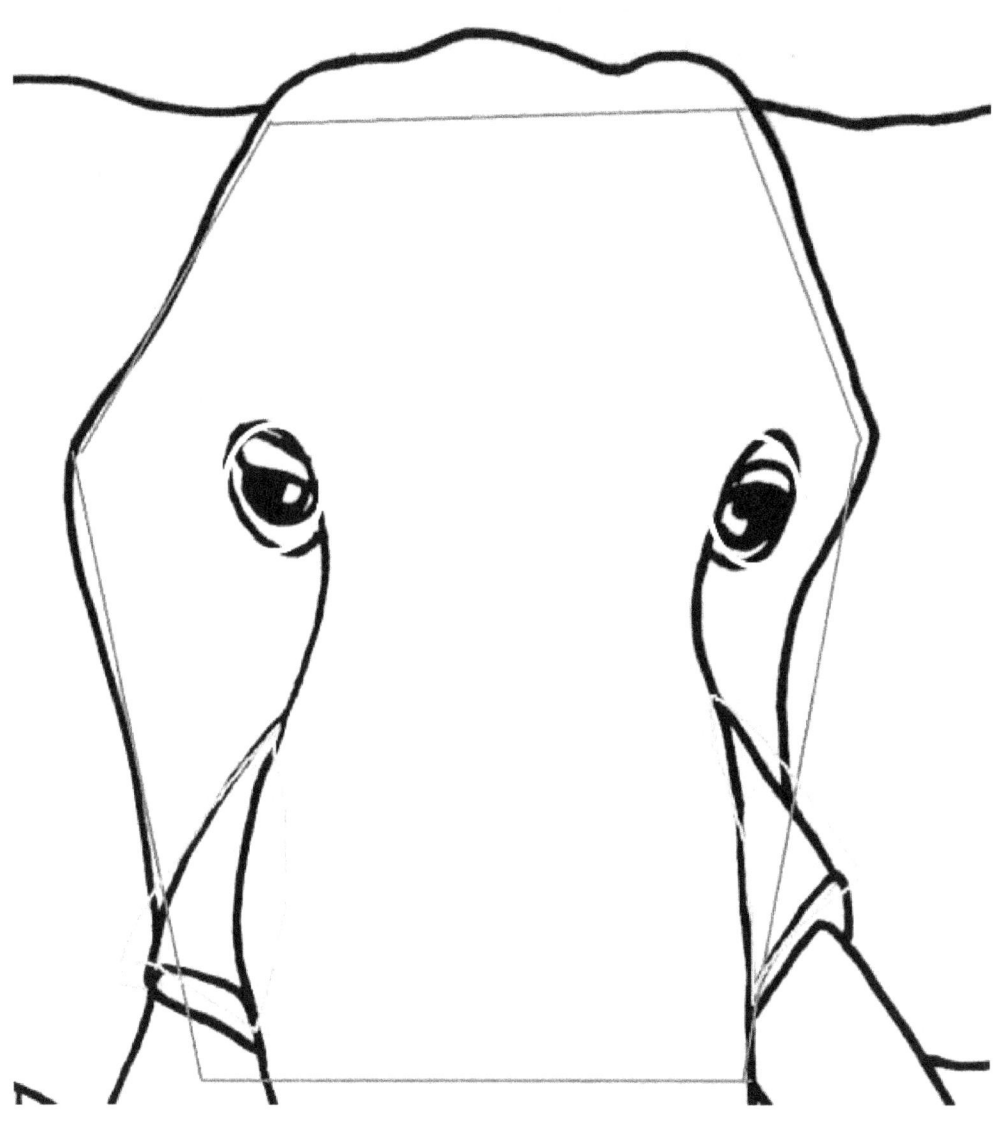

Step three: Let us leave the tusks and go back to the hexagonal shaped head. In the middle part up draw two circles near each opposite side-there you can then work on the eyes-.

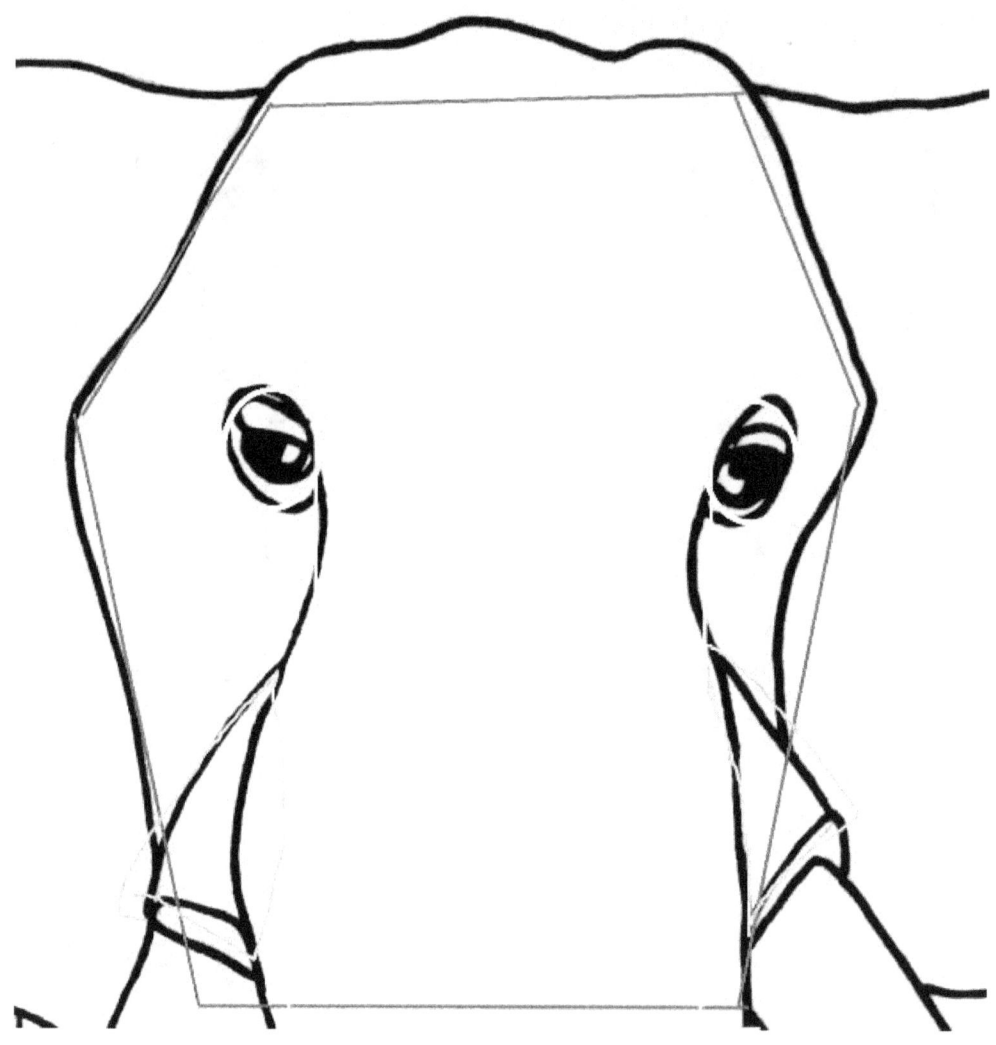

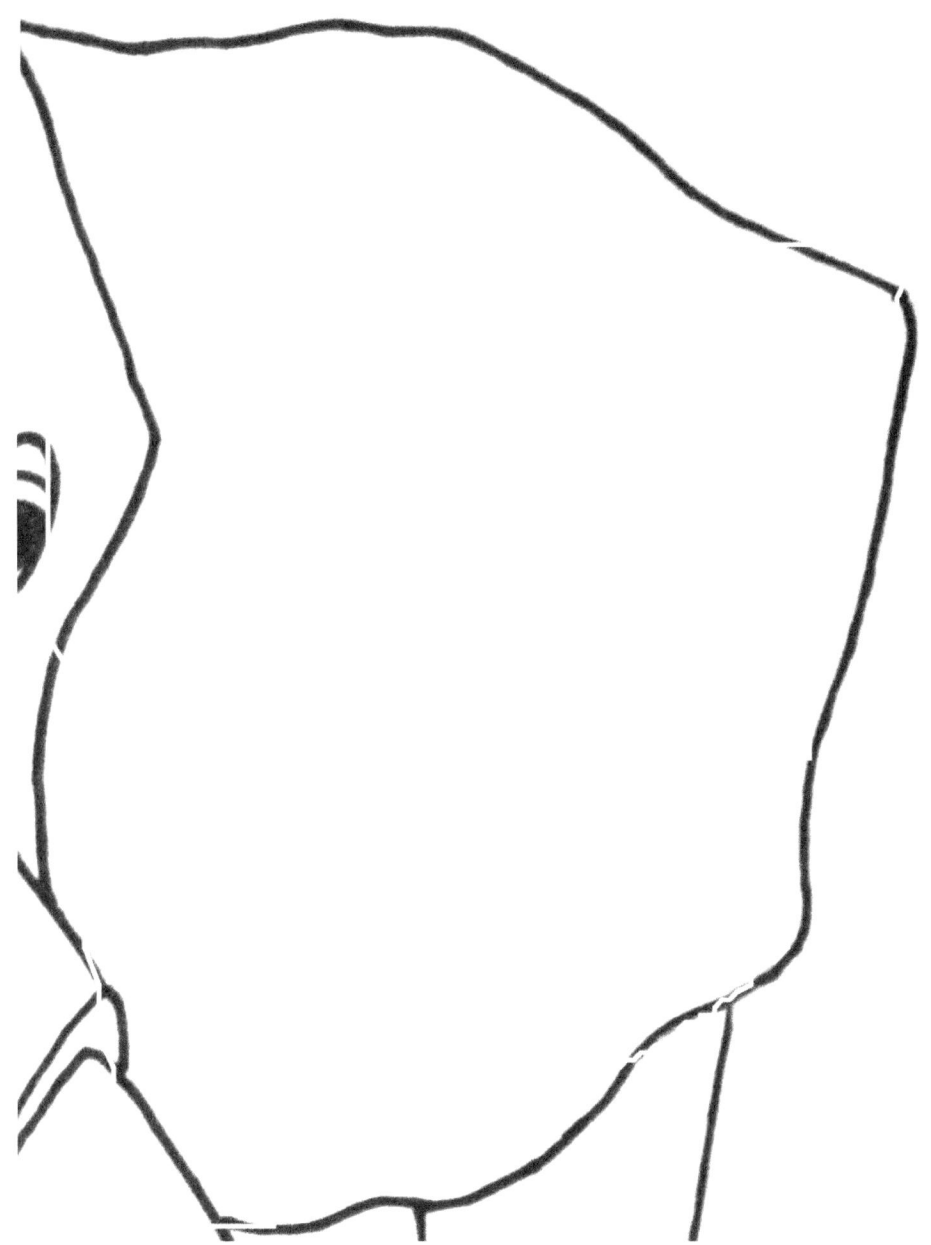

Step four: For the trump you can draw to irregular lines at a good distance of each other; draw them as they separate more and more in different directions. Strike the strokes as if they were curvilinear.

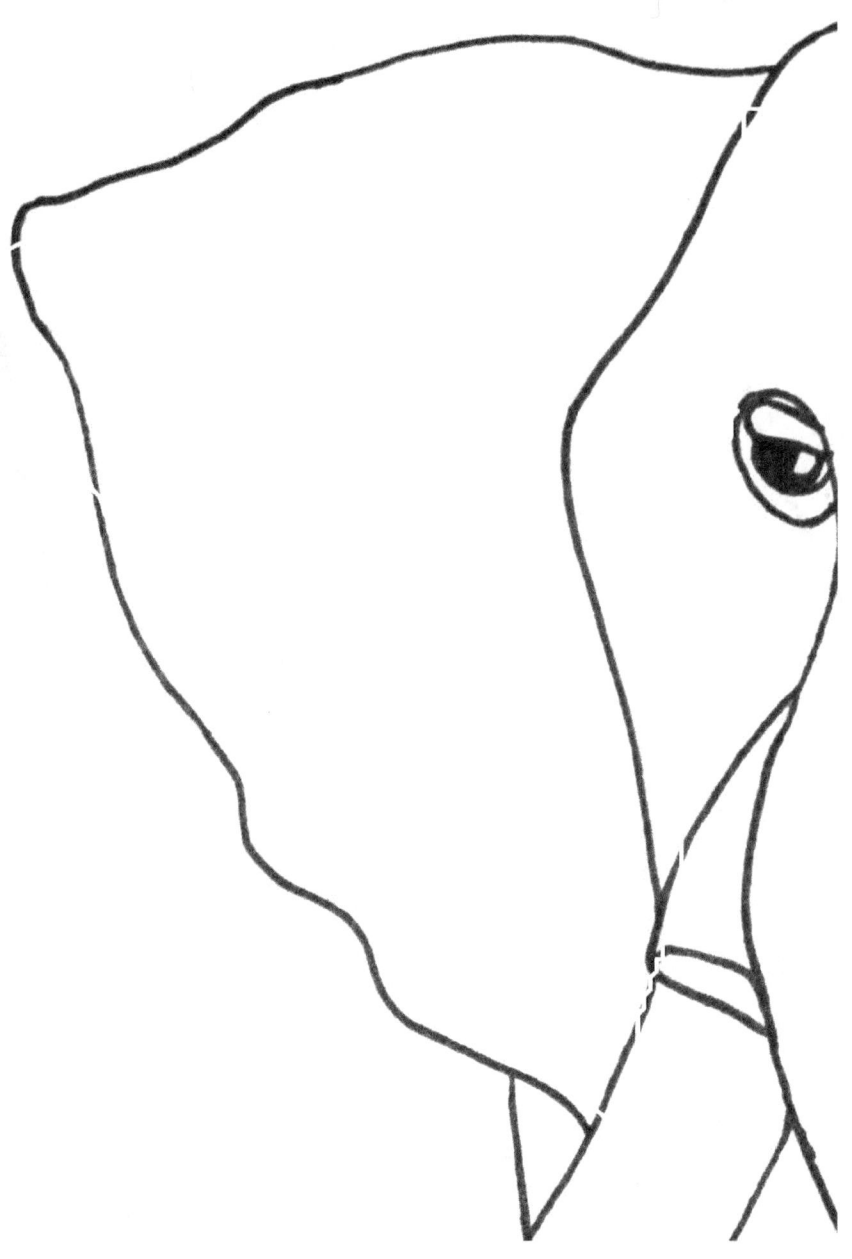

Step five: For the ears we are working with triangles, of a big size. Draw them taking on account that they are born from the sides of the head; so respect the silhouette of it when making the ears. Do the strokes as irregular as you can manage.

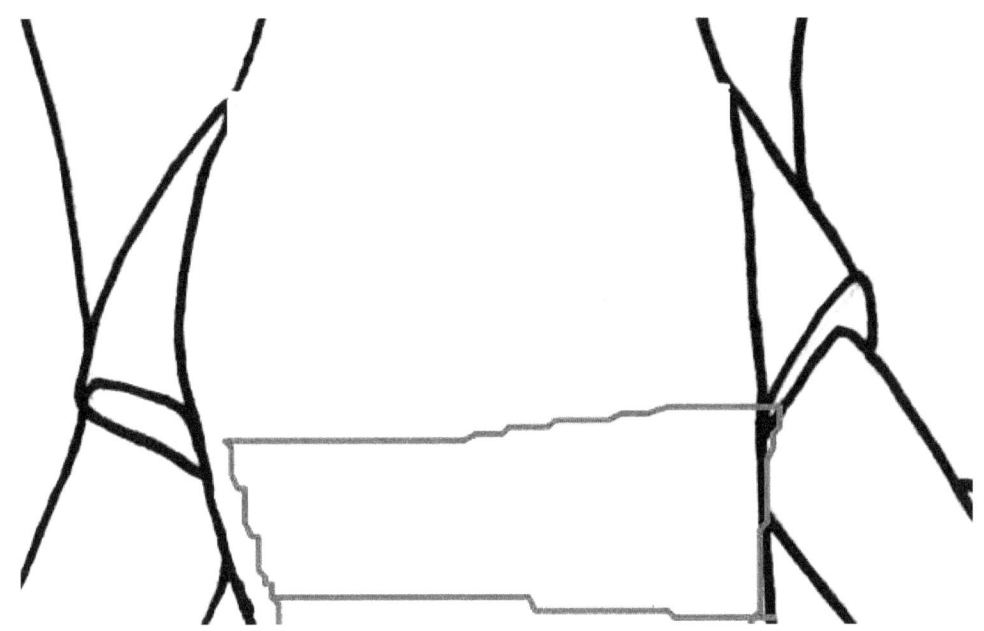

Step six: Now we are returning to the trump. Look at the shape: it is composed of two trapezoid looking forms, one in reverse of the other; the one on top also is considerably bigger that the one down. You can use these internal shapes in case if just drawing lines separating from each other didn't work well.

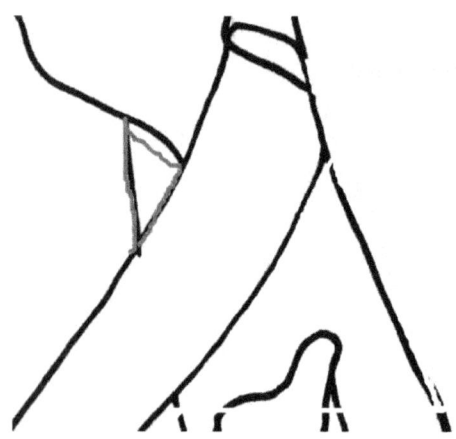 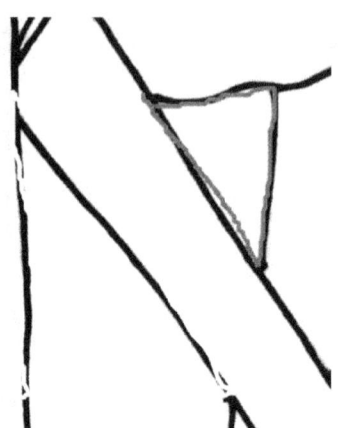

Step seven: To mark the distance from the trump to the tusks and from them to the ears we are using triangles, which not only serves to mark the separation, but also to mark the outlines. From the trump to the tusks the triangle in a normal position, while from the ears to the tusks they are considerably smaller and upside down.

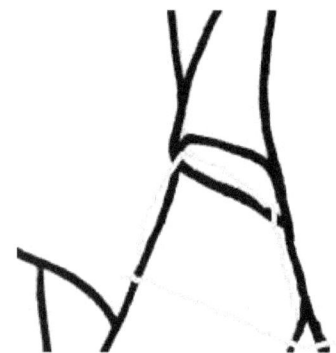 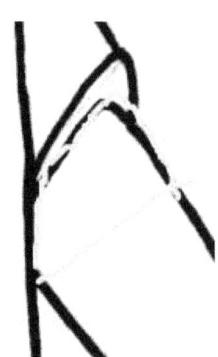

Step eight: The tusks are quite easy to make, we have two trapezoids, one at each side of the trump, to start. After that, just scribble some lines, four in total, and two for each tusk. The lines will go down drawing curves with opposite directions that will culminate in a triangle-as it seen above-.

Continuing with the picture, notice how our elephant is moving forward, facing us. To get this effect we need just to show three of the four legs. To create the limbs we will be using basic geometrical forms, to be precise: trapezoids, from the bottom to the top. The first two are one slightly tinier than the other. Next comes the ones that are upside down. It will look kind alike a sand hourglass with a wide center, that will grow wider and wider as it goes to the body.

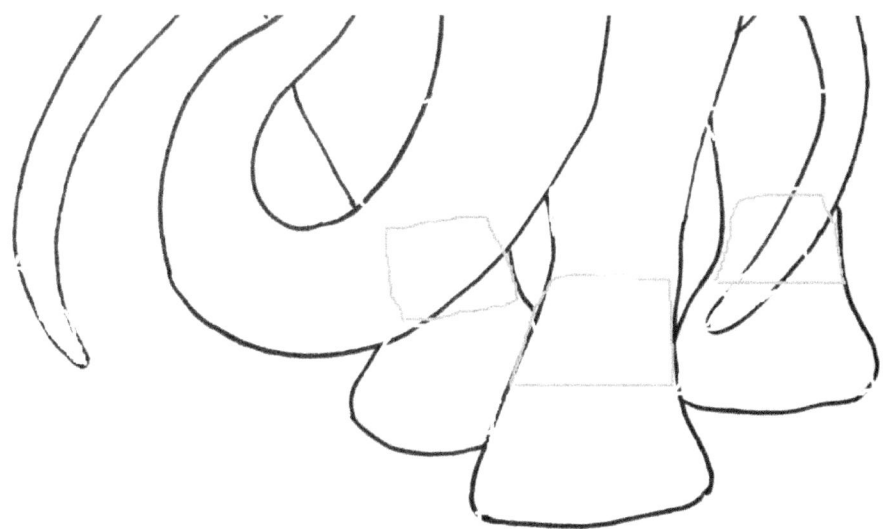

Put the trump and one of the tusks in front of the legs; coming back to the extremities, put the one in the front in a bigger size, then put one a bit more inclined than the other-that way it emulates motion-. The trump will be drawn curled to one side, with the nostrils facing up and visible.

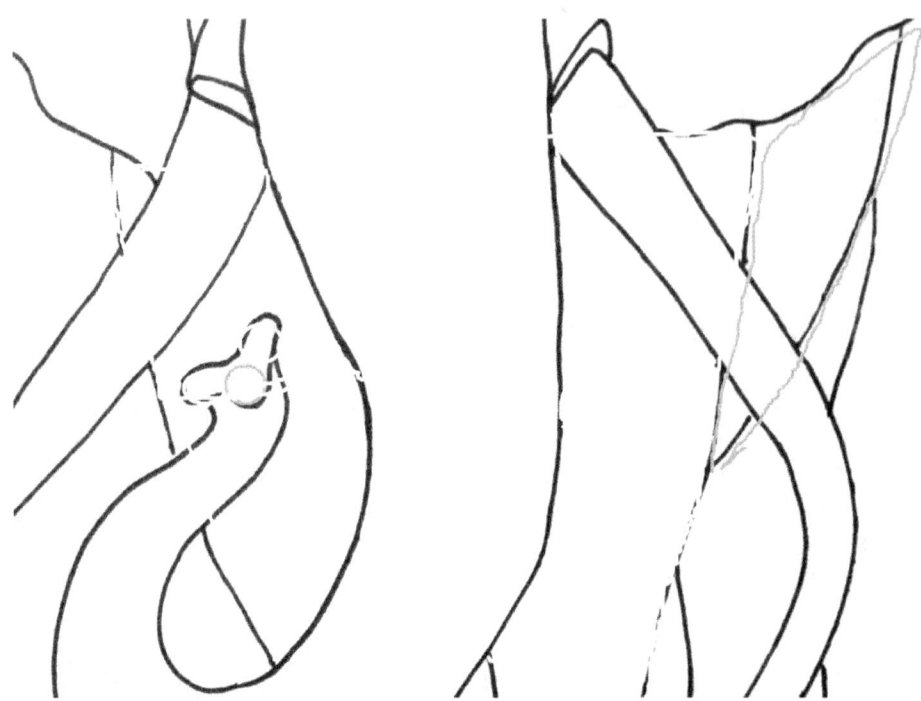

Step nine: The limbs of the pachyderm are more vertically like than any other mammal to support their own weight; in this case, this does not matter here although, because we will be constructing the stumps with trapezoids and triangles, as it is seen above. Notice how the extremities are behind the trump and the tusks. For the nostrils use three circles and put them as a triangle.

Now that we have make every part of the mammal, using mostly triangles and trapezoids, lets us take a few steps back to see the entire being. Following the instructions you should have been able to get something that looks like this:

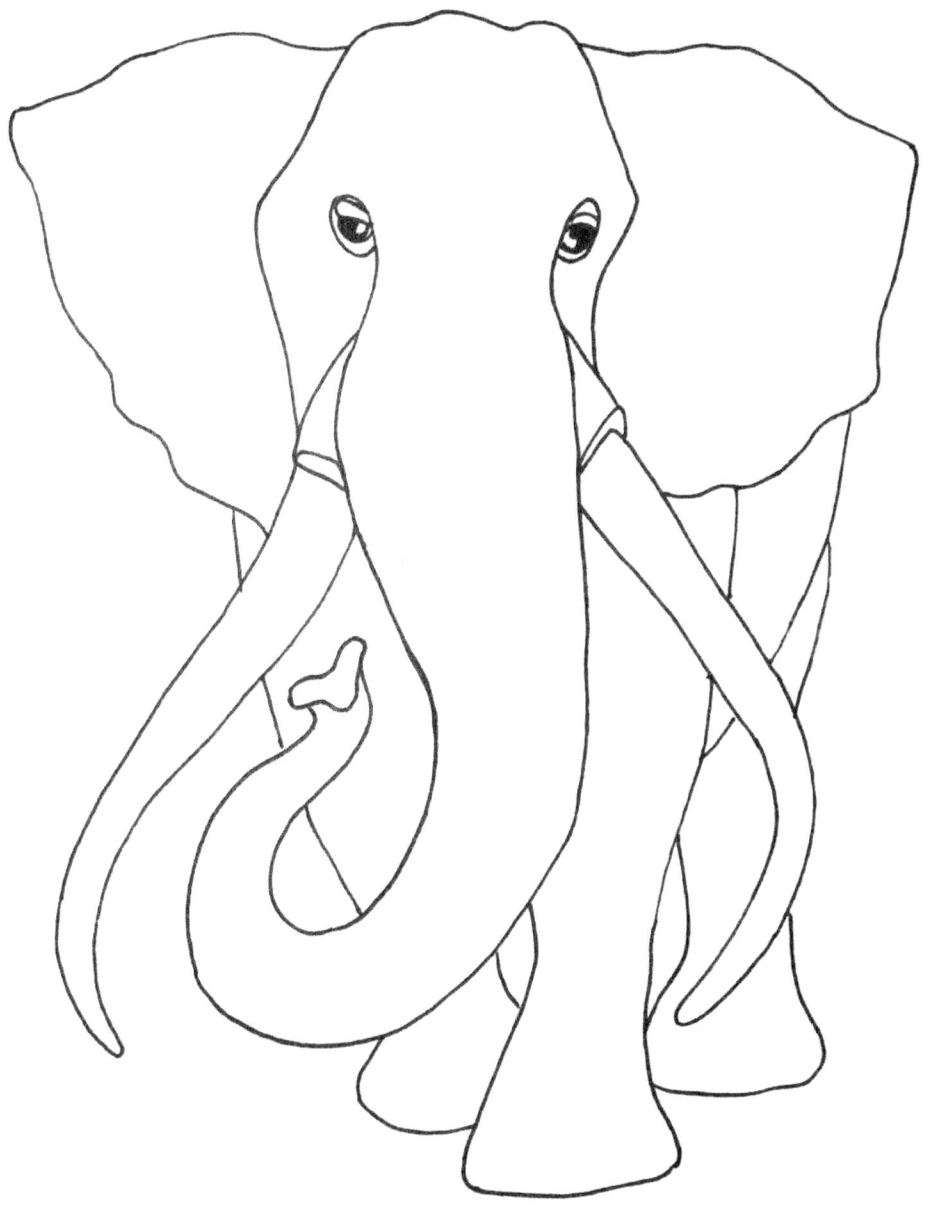

You did it! Great! Now let us continue; this is just the start of the lesson.

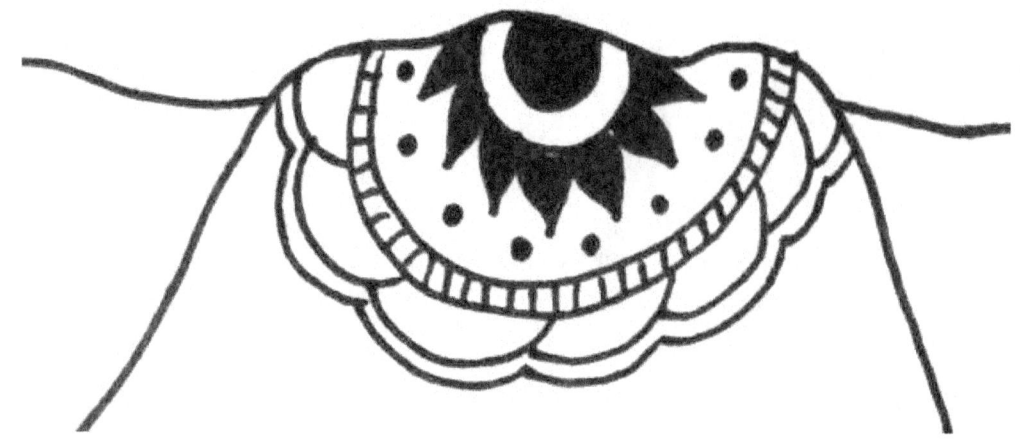

Step ten: We will locate ourselves inside the top of the tuskers head. Draw four semicircles one inside the other with the one nearest to the top being the smaller one. Ink the first one; after this leave a space, that create the second circle. Continuing from this, make various triangles going one next to another following a disk like shape; after this base is done outline curved lines for the contour of the triangles. Then put small points in the space between each one-. Also notice how the void has the shape of a triangle-. So looking back we have what looks like a sun surrounded by small circles.

After this draw two lines parallel to the other in an arch, draw horizontal strokes one next to the other respects the outlines of the arches. Now for the last semi ring form, draw one small semicircle, one after the other, then draw a curvilinear line following the outlines of the little semicircles.

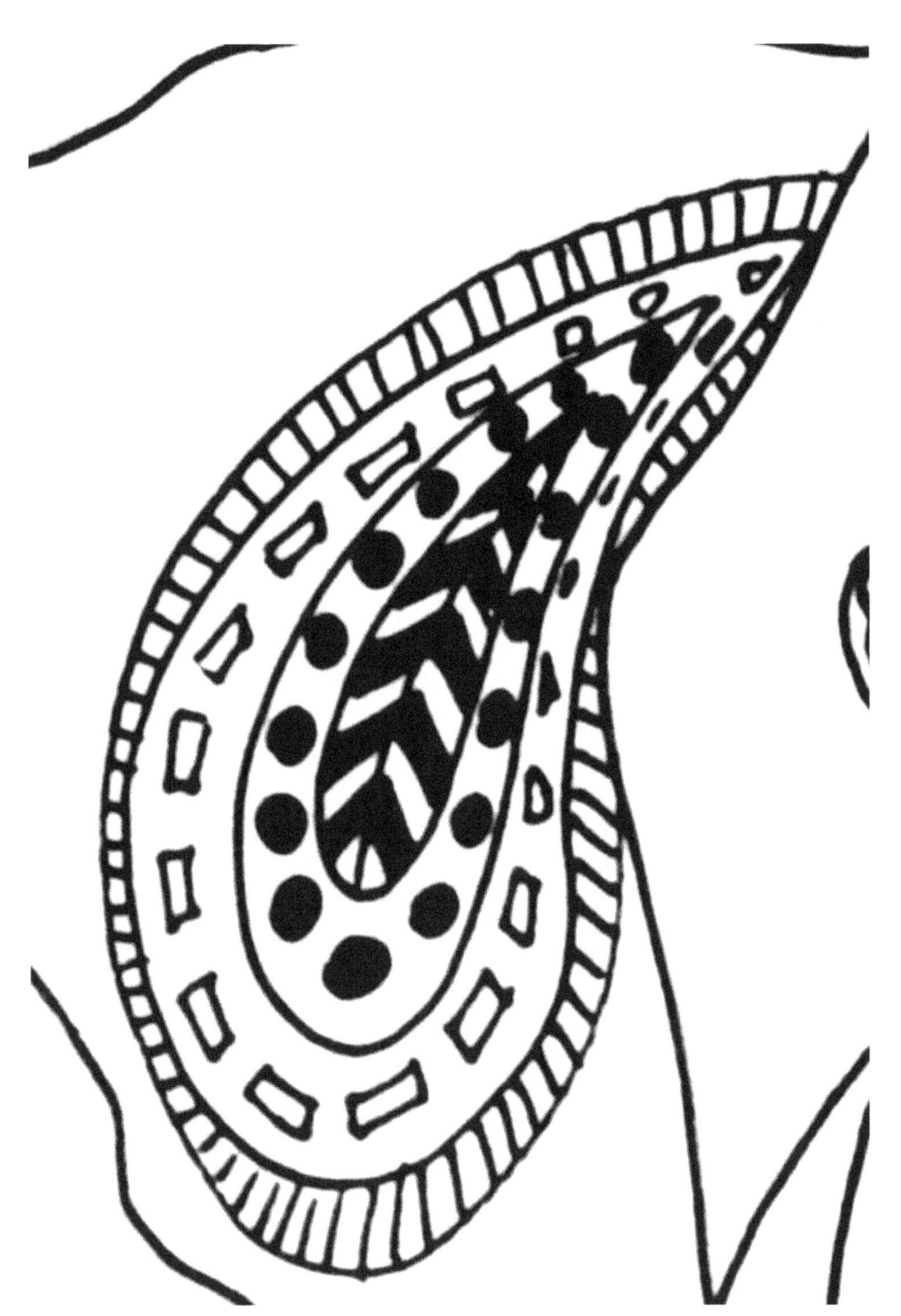

Step eleven: This one is really simple, it is like a big peacock feather, or more precisely one peacock motif inside the other. The outlier will have a coexistent equal, just a bit apart to each other, with aligned horizontal lines inside the void between them. Then following the shape draw various rectangles; in the next space make various big circles, ink them. For the last space divide the figure with a line, and draw diagonal lines going on opposing directions one right down the other, ink every other one.

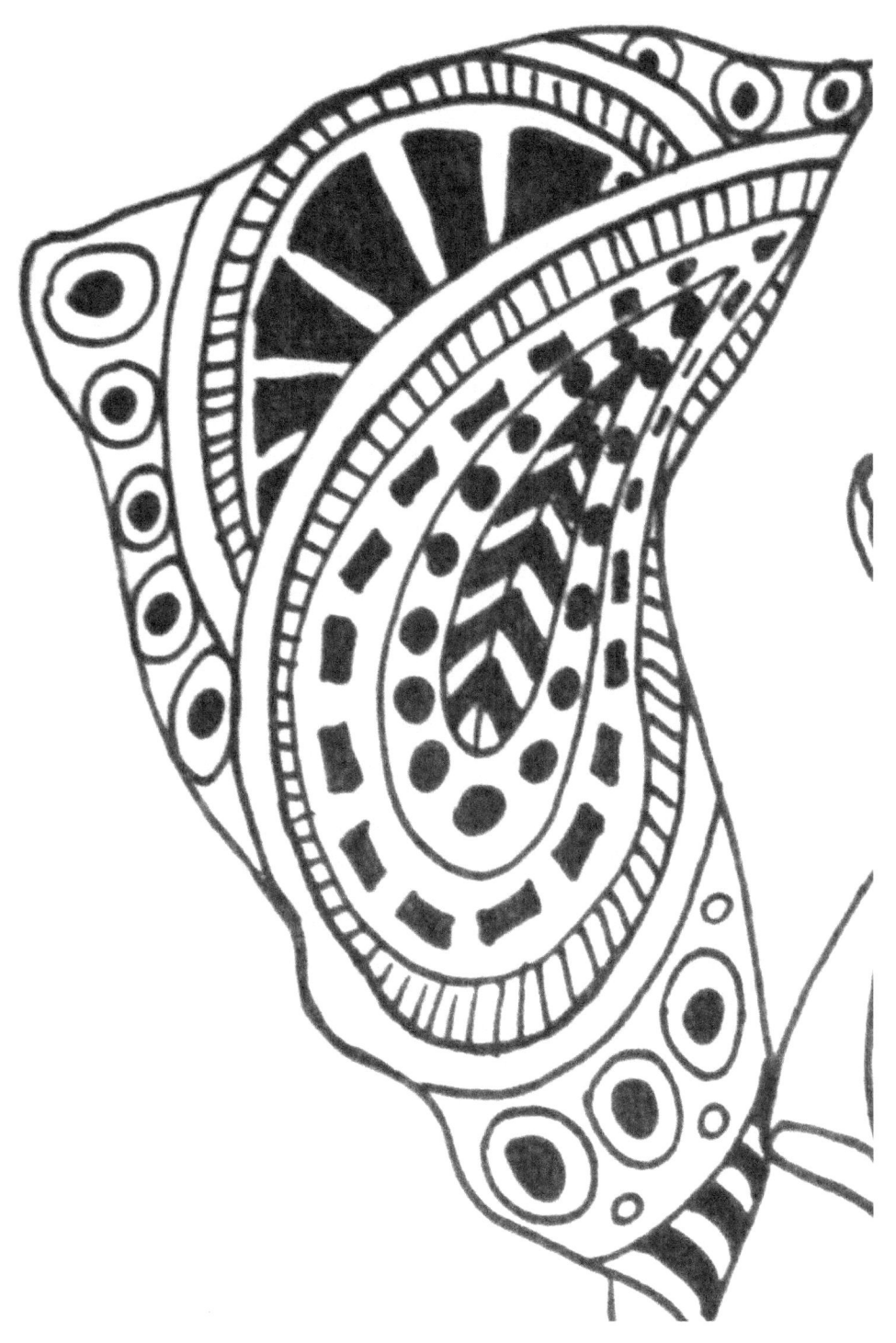

Step twelve: Near to the start of the tusk, in the ear draw a trigonal form, draw one vertical line next to the other, with seven lines one slightly apart from the other, in every other space between two lines leave it empty, painting black the remaining ones.

In the space above, draw three large circles with smaller inked ones inside of them; also sketch two small empty points between the first circle, the center, the last circle and the center. We fly over the peacock motif, we situate ourselves on the top part of the ear; draw an arch that will surpass the outlines of the ear.

Next to it make another semicircle and another- try to make each one smaller than the other-; in the space between the second and third draw vertical strokes one after the other. In the gap between the third semicircle and the place with the peacock motif we will be making upside triangles that will converge in the center (we recommend to do this first with pencil, because it will be needed to erase the points), draw seven of this figures, once it is done ink them.

Now you will notice that there are two free spaces, one near the head and the other on the other side, following the outline of the biggest arc draw various circles with smaller inked ones inside them.

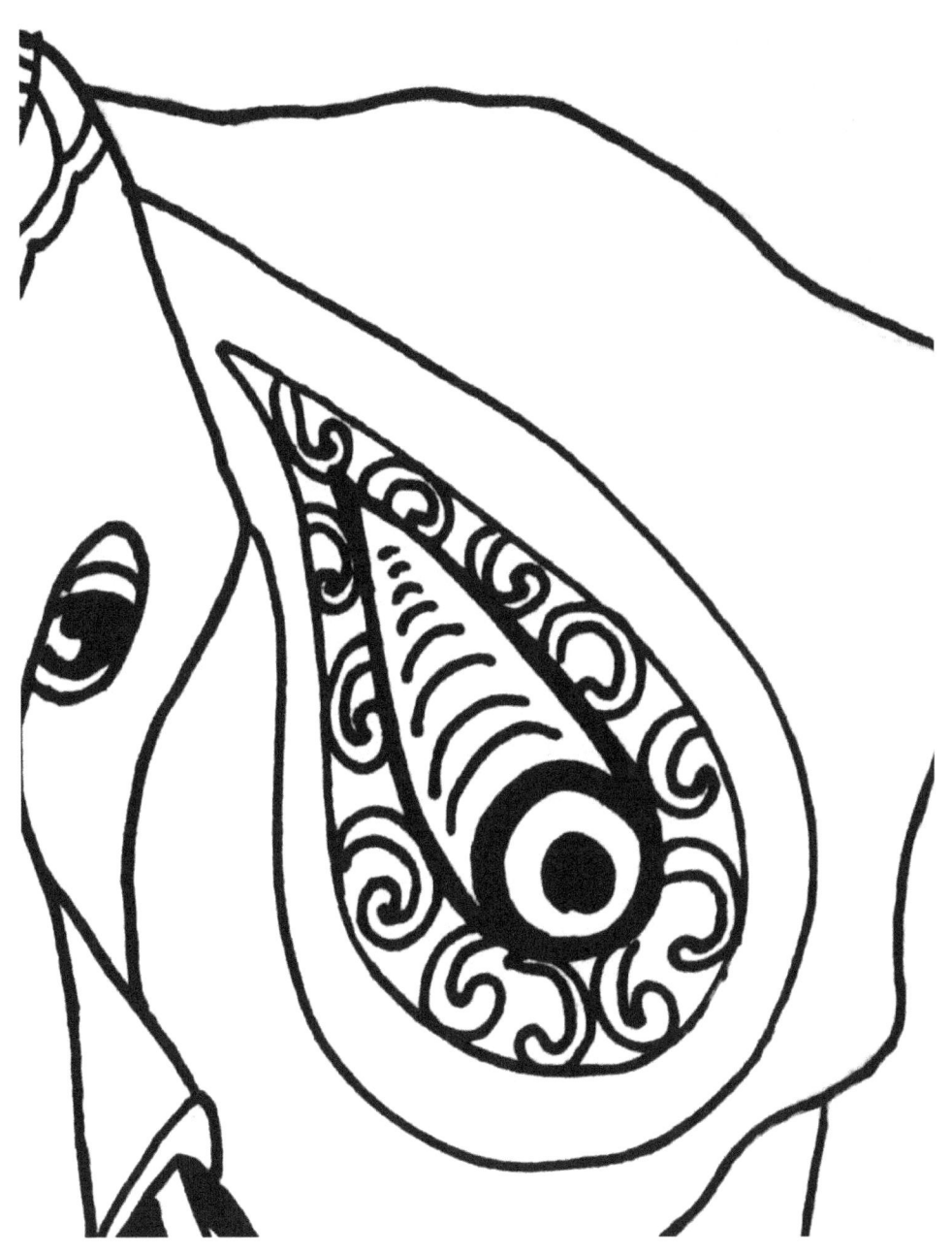

Step thirteen: Now we are moving to the other ear; and again we start with another outline that looks like a peacock's plumage, after sketching this, draw one huge water drop inside of it. Make a thick line for the gout; with this same thickness make an outline for a circle with another one inside it that will be painted black.

Remaining inside the drop, draw various arcs following the decreasing size of the form and the direction of the circle. In the space between the drop and the peacock feather outline start drawing various double lined curls with this order: every other one will be upside down.

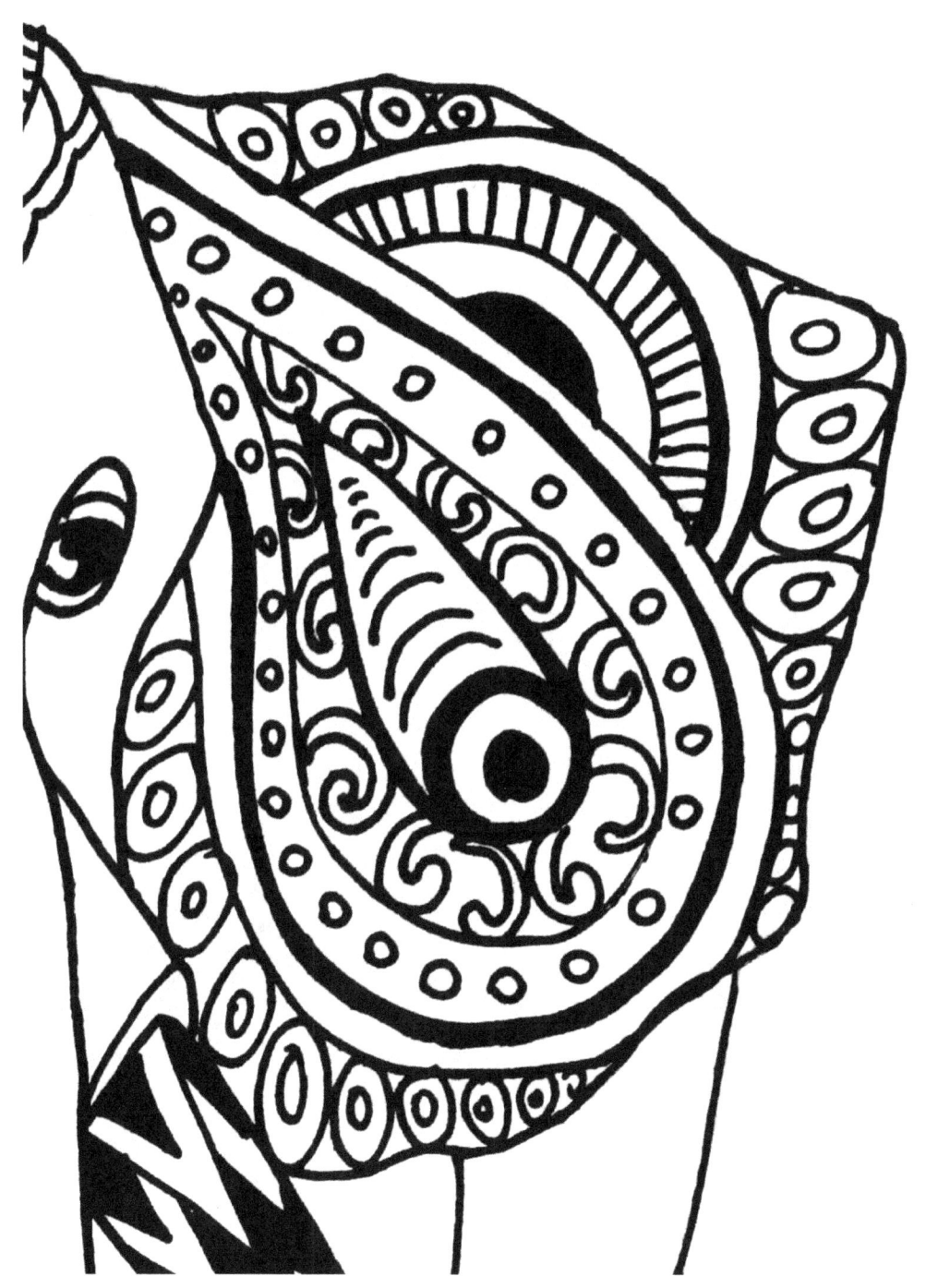

Step fourteen: Now continuing with the peacock motive, draw a parallel outline with a thicker line, leaving a considerable space, so little empty circles can be sketched inside the area. In the bottom part of the ear draw ellipses with circles inside of them, respecting the outline of the thick line we just talk about, giving some air between this drawing and the line.

Moving up we will be doing the same semicircular shape that we already described one step back- the one that looks like a cut orange-, only that now we will replace the upside down triangles with only one inked arc inside. Repeat the process aforementioned for the circles and ellipses with smaller circles inside.

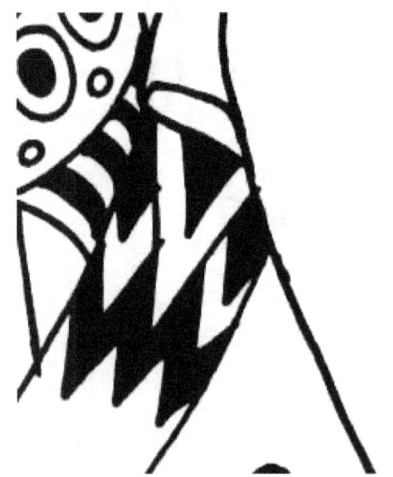 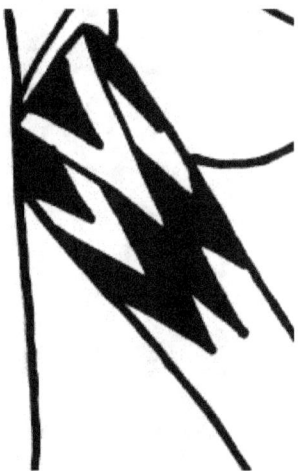

Step fifteen: This is quite simple, the first part of the tusks is formed inside by various triangles; the center one is inked, with one empty one that is bigger springing from behind, the other two triangles on the sides of the middle one are also inked and have their respective empty bigger figures behind; right after this there will be yet another set of three inked triangles.

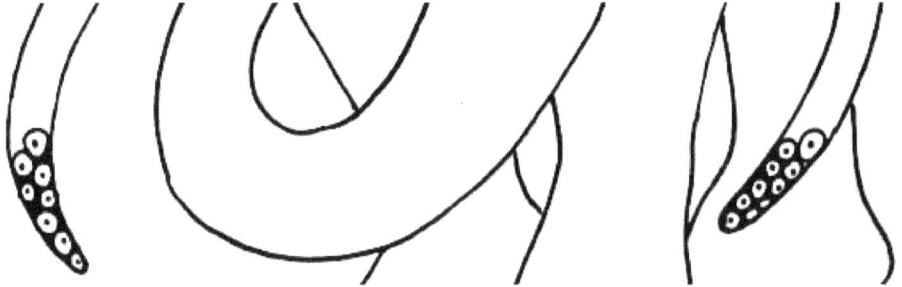

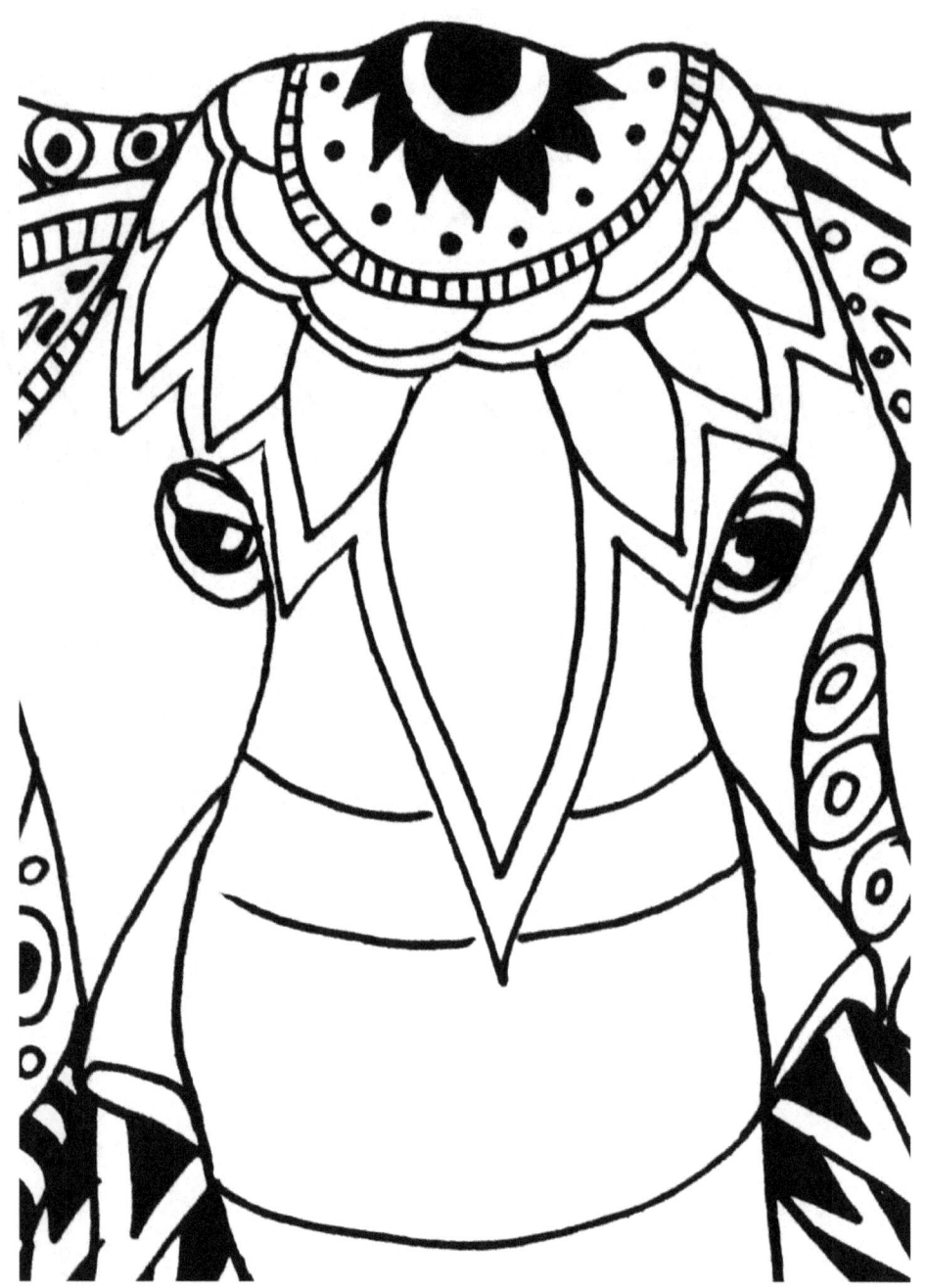

Step sixteen: On the point of the tusks draw small circles with points inside of them.

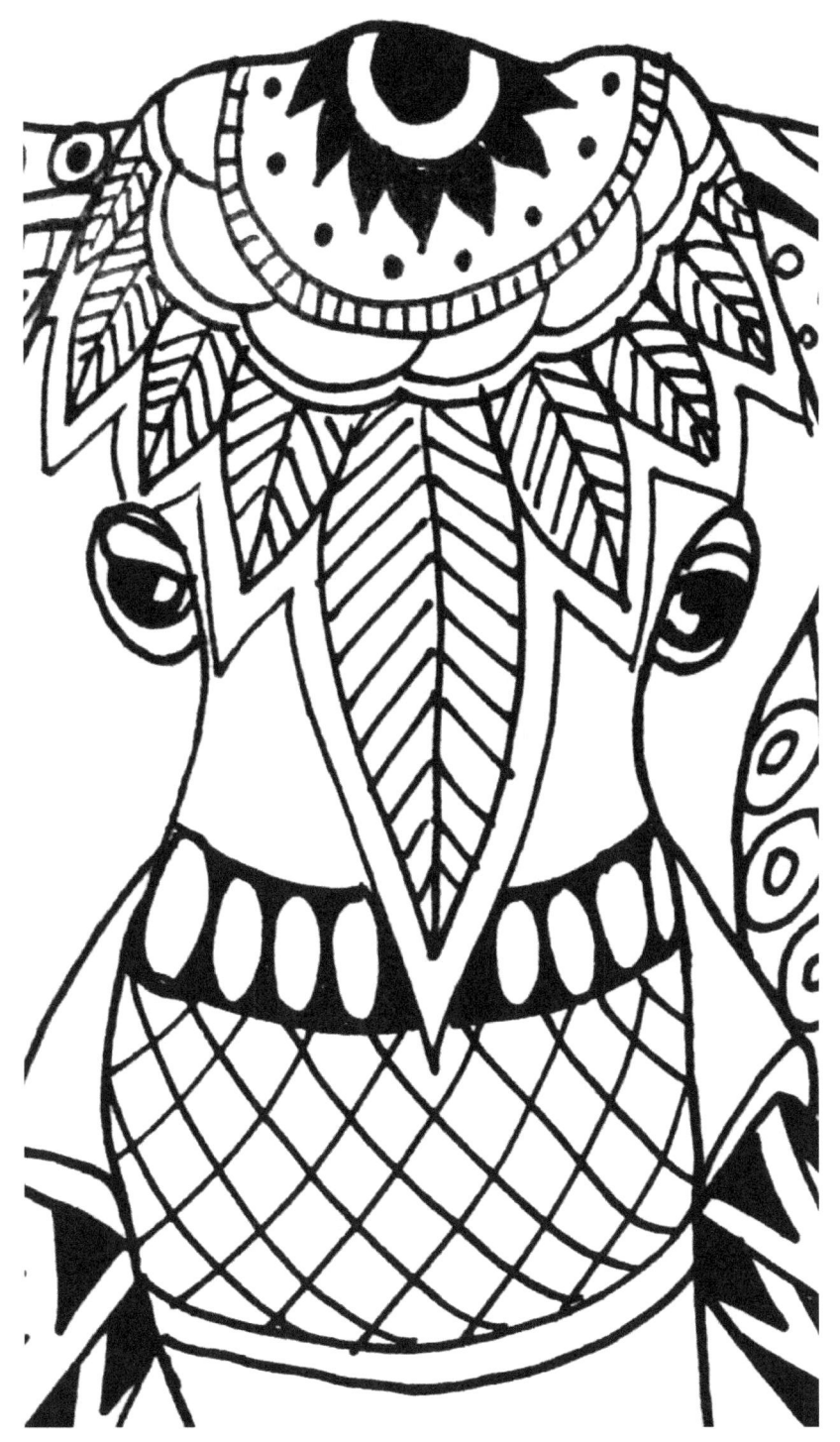

Step seventeen: Let us go back to the drawing made way back on Step ten. From the semicircles we will start making various petals that will end in a point, with one huge one in the middle of the arc. Move down to the beginning of the trump, draw three curved lines, the first two in the area with the point of the big petal, the third curve should be draw quite apart from the other two.

Step eighteen: We will concentrate first on the petal shape forms, inside each of them make one line in the middle, after that draw diagonal lines that will converge in the middle, the direction will be pointing to the semicircle on top. Draw an outline following the format of the leaflets. Next start inking the space between the two curves we have already made; paint the space in a way that blank spaces with the shape of ovals will be in there too. Then draw a net between the second and third curve- it will look like various rhombs-.

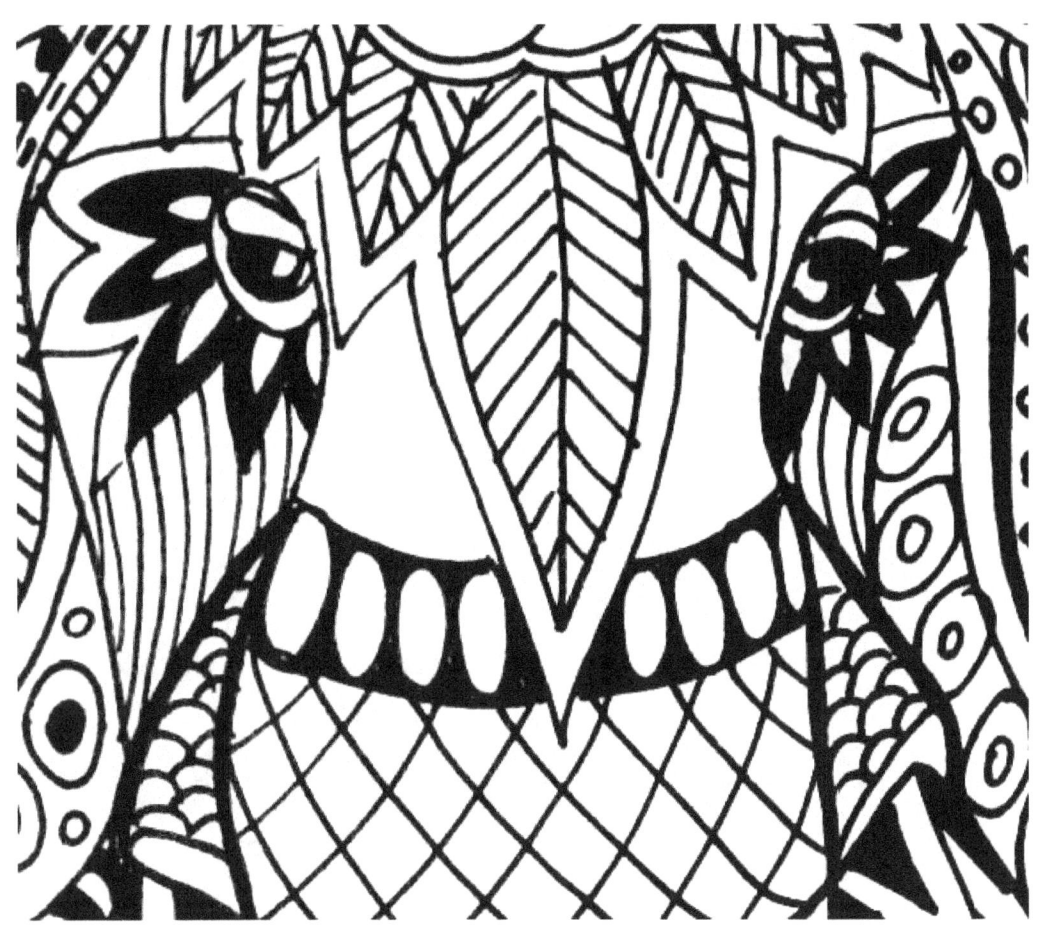

Step nineteen: Look at the sides of the trump, make flakes with arcs. Then above each of them draw vertical lines; use the silhouette of leafs to draw very broad lines following the form mentioned earlier.

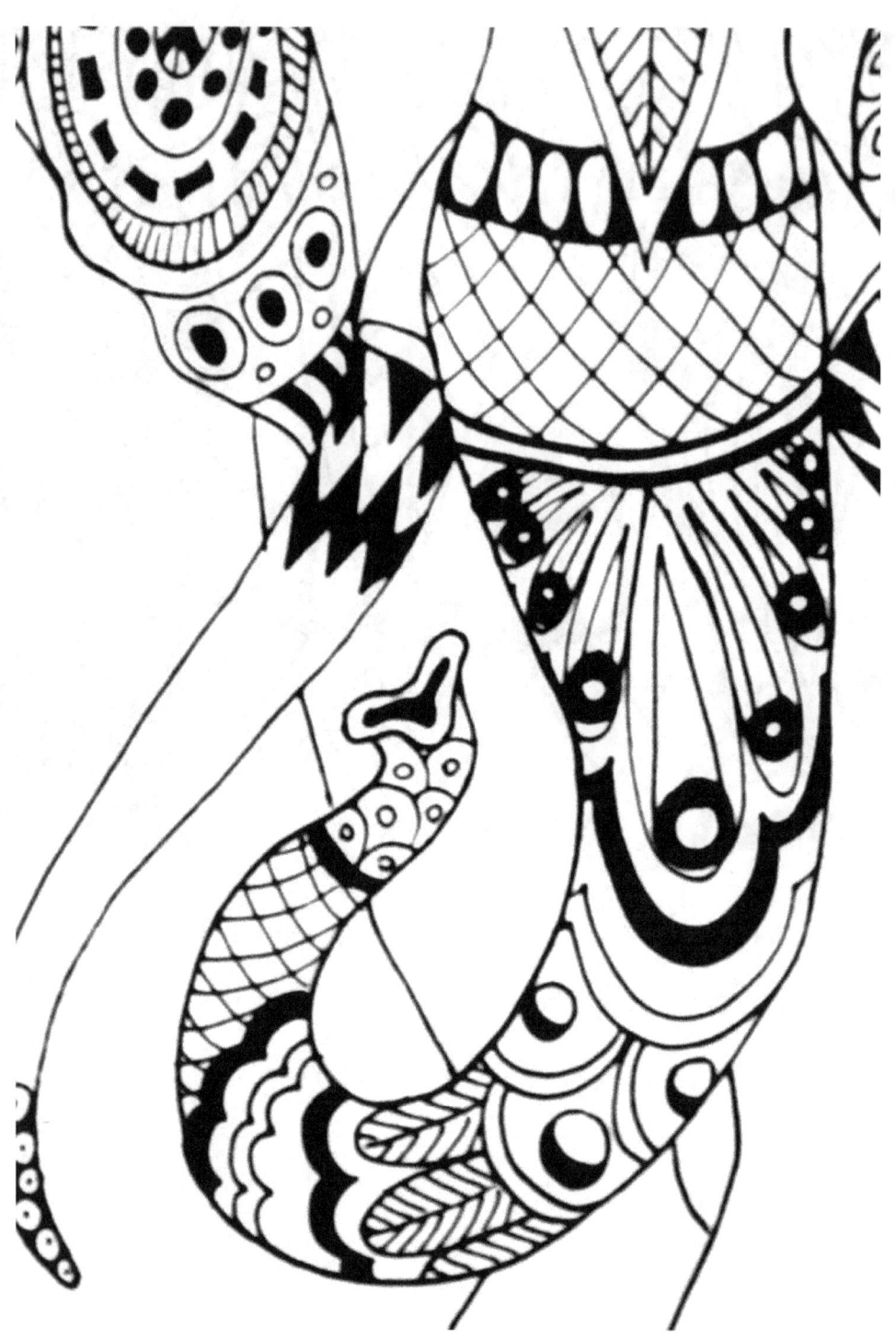

Step twenty: We will start with the trump - draw seven or so drops, with triangles inside each of them, also with a circle inside them. Sketch a wide outline that follows the pattern of the various drops, leave an empty space, then repeat the process making another thick line, and only this time leave it without ink.

After this, use three arcs, looking like flakes, inside make circles with a half-moon painted black inside them; also do a double line for the arcs. The next thing to do will be to draw three big leafs, with broad black outlines following the shape formed by them, leave some space and do the same, only making two parallel shapes, another space, and then a thick inked one.

Draw a net that will end in an encounter with a broad curve; then make semicircles that will reminiscent of flakes, with small circles inside. For the nostril paint the inside space black.

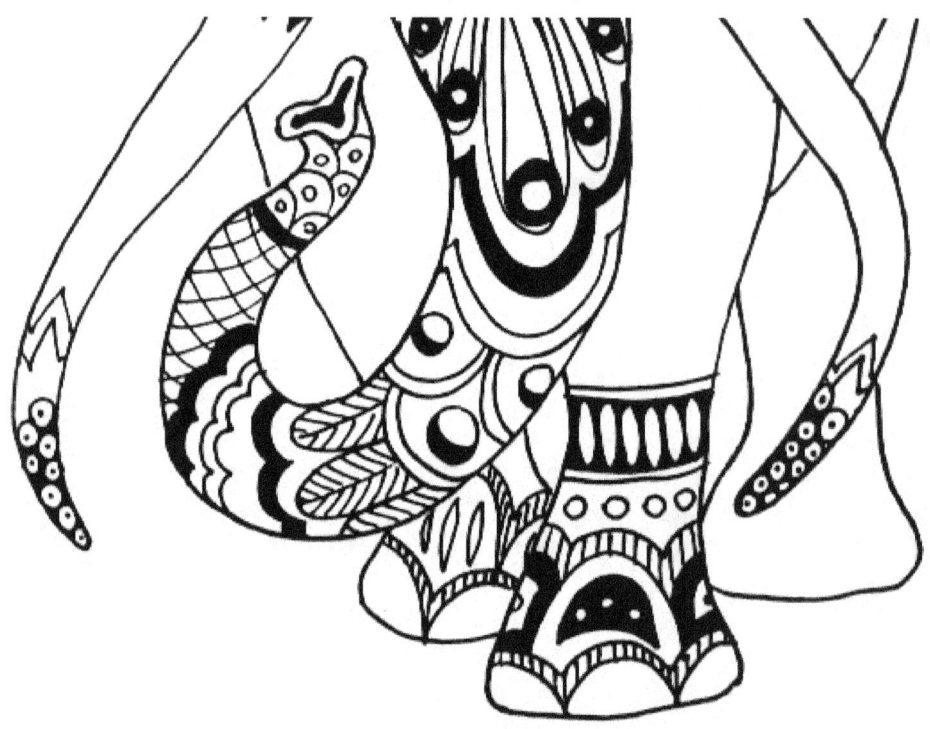

Step twenty one: Now we are moving to the limbs, starting with the one up front. From the bottom up, draw three arcs one next to the other, make another set of these, join them with vertical lines; repeat this ,leaving a big space between them, so you can draw different forms inside the void- in this case, it is another arched form that is used, with the middle one being white black in white and the others being the opposite-.

On the top, make four horizontal lines with a huge separation between each pair; in between draw large ovals, leaving them white and painting black the remaining space. Following this move to the closest paw, where we will be drawing another set of parallel arcs, with vertical strokes between them; leave an empty space to draw oval like shapes-three of them-, and up those repeat the process for the arcs drawn before.

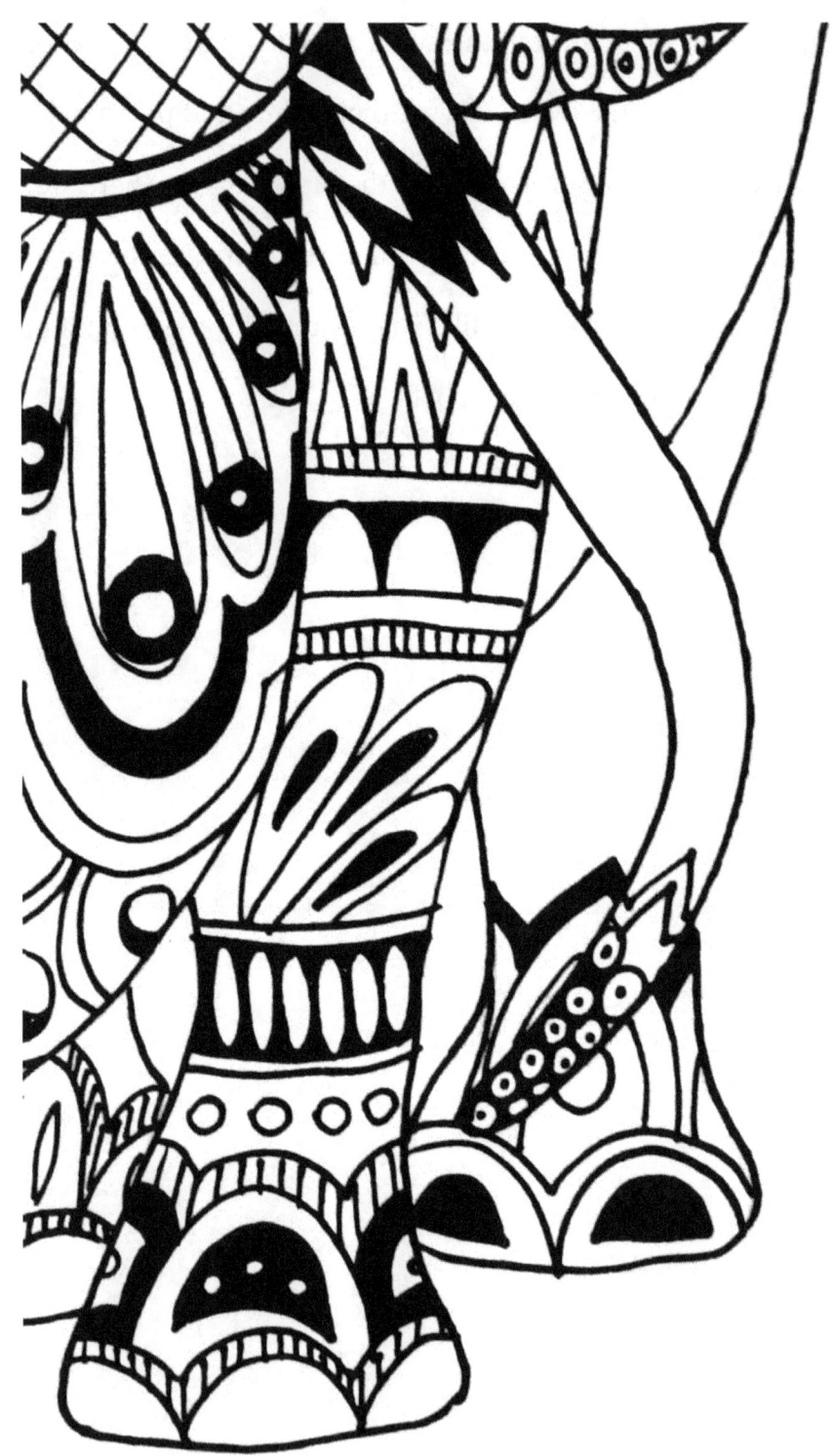

Step twenty two: Let us go back to the center limb, now draw three drop like figures with a diagonal direction, draw smaller drops inside of each one, and then color them black. Draw a pair of parallel horizontal lines across the limb; add vertical lines inside the space between them. Separated from this, draw another horizontal line, then sketch three semicircles with another line above them, fill the space between the line and the arcs with black. Leave another space, draw another pair of horizontal lines and start making various long triangles one inside and side by side the other.

Then move to the third extremity, there the process of drawing two semicircles at the bottom with two smaller ones painting them black; draw an outline following the shape of these arcs. Above this draw vertical curved lines encountering in the middle, with other two in opposite directions, inside the space, the middle curvatures make an empty circle. Draw a thick black line following the scheme formed by the figures just below.

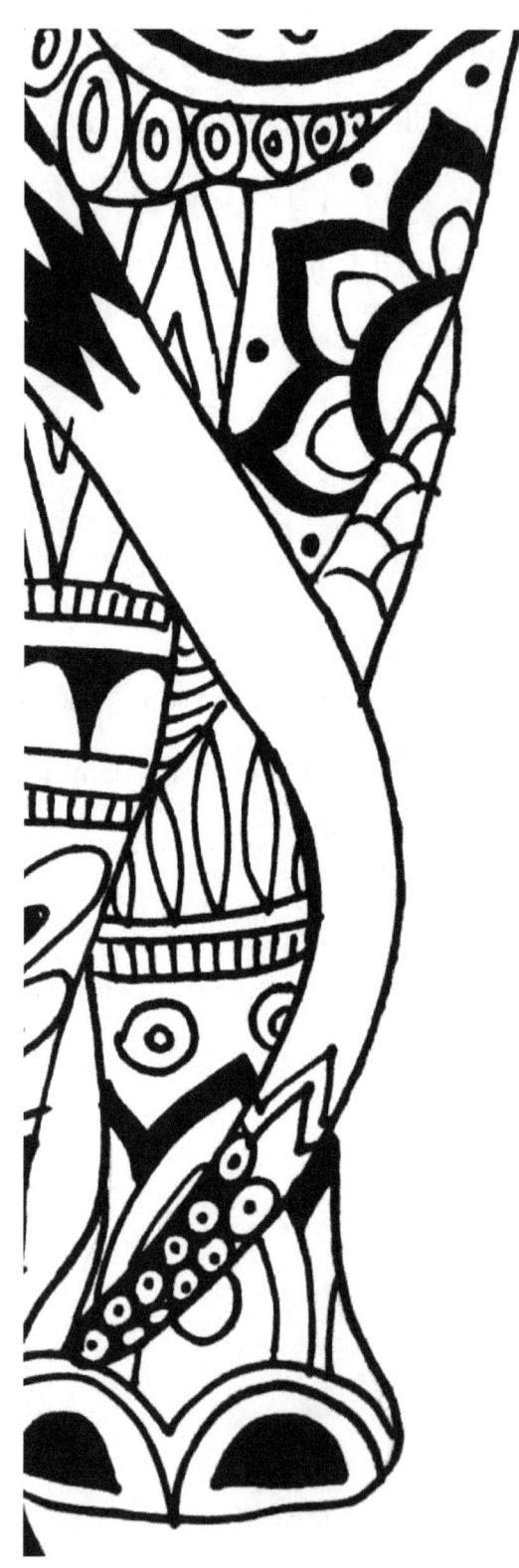

Step twenty three:

Continuing from the last step, draw another set of two horizontal lines and above them, make curved lines vertically set. In the upper part of the limb draw some flakes. Then move to the visible part of the body and in the space between the lower part and the tusk draw some curved lines. Above the tusk draw a figure similar to the one on top of the head of the elephant, the one that looks either like a flower or a stylistic sun; put black points in the space between each petal.

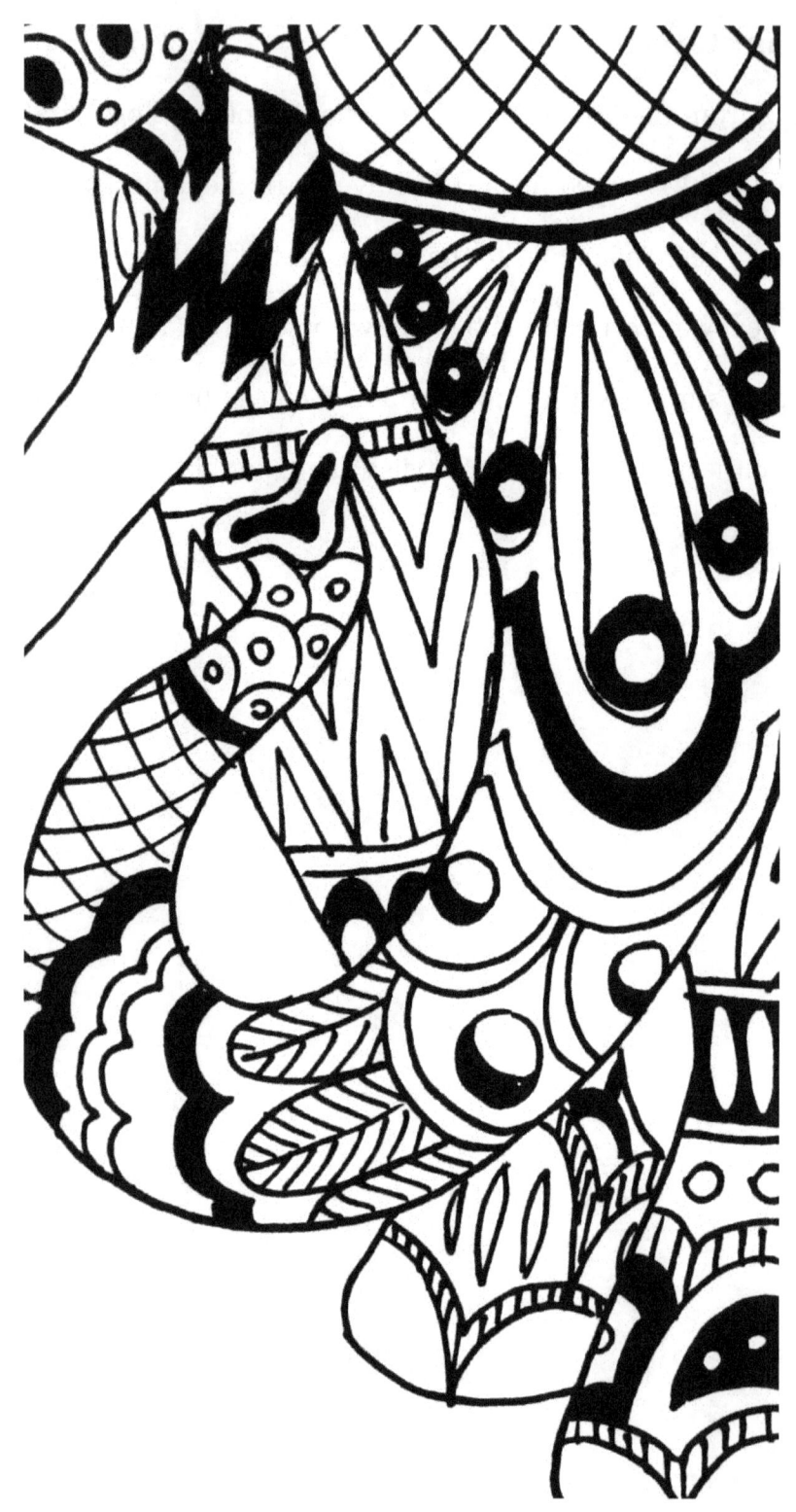

Step twenty four: Now we are going to repeat familiar - steps a pair of parallel arcs joined with vertical lines; a space, another pair of semicircles, with the same thing. Draw thick black flakes; draw various triangles as base above two horizontal lines, then make a double lined double u; make four horizontal lines above that. Make oval thin shapes inside the empty space. Between the second and third line make some vertical lines one alongside the other.

Finally, we will be getting this:

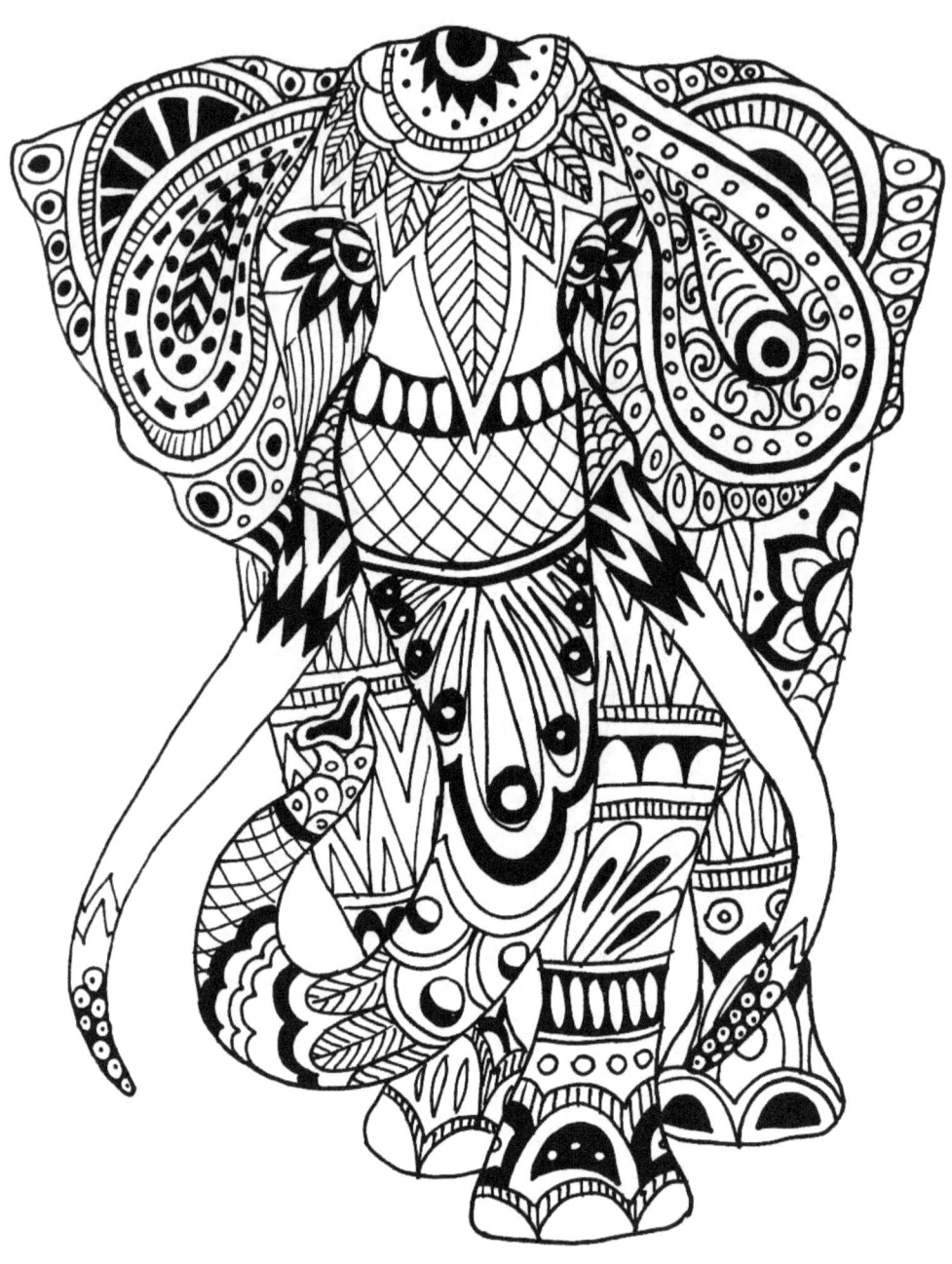

Drawing level 2: That is one curious giraffe.

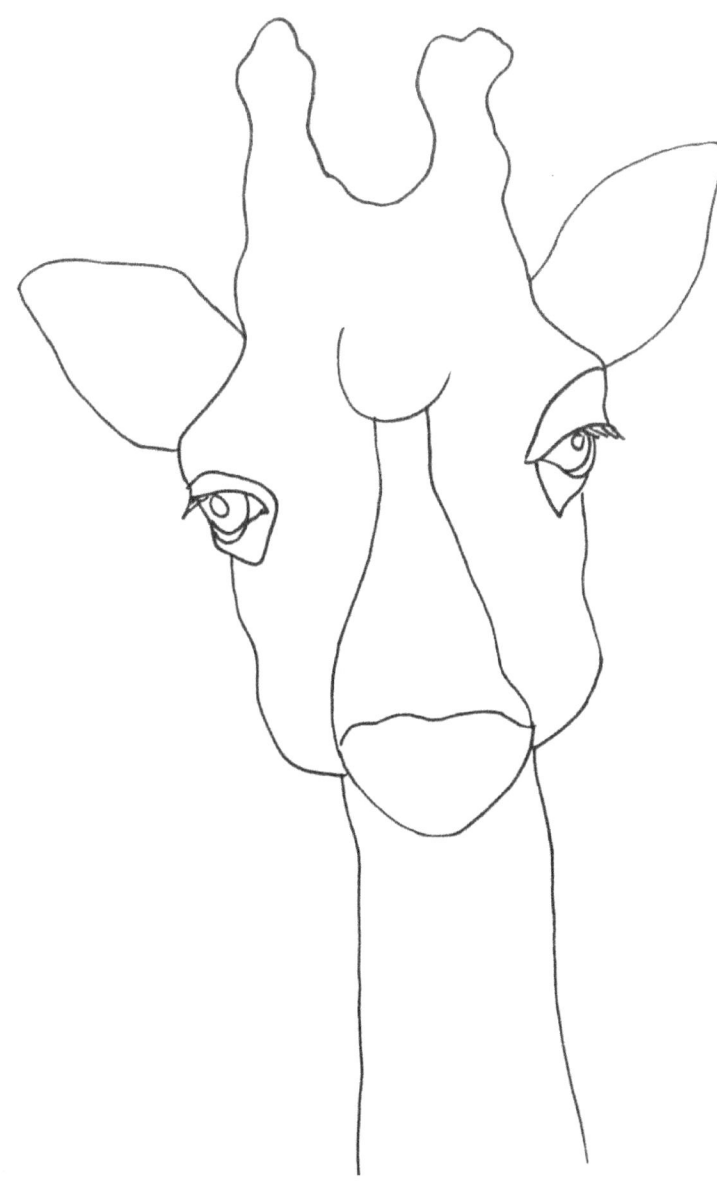

Step one: We are continuing with another mammal, the giraffe. Notice how irregular the lines are. Let us begin with the neck, the easiest part by far; it is just two parallel vertical lines far apart from the other, sketch swirly lines with a small inclination to the center point.

Next we move up, and as in the prior exercise we use a hexagon as a base for the face; surpassing the base draw an upside down triangle; just above it draw a taller triangle that will be truncated with a curvature. To do the eyes you must locate yourself in each horizontal extreme of the face, draw two half rhombuses, add two horizontally drops, and two arcs-one from each eye-. Continuing with the two extremes, let go to the ears - the shape will be similar to the leafs. The giraffe horns can be acquired with a big M shaped figure.

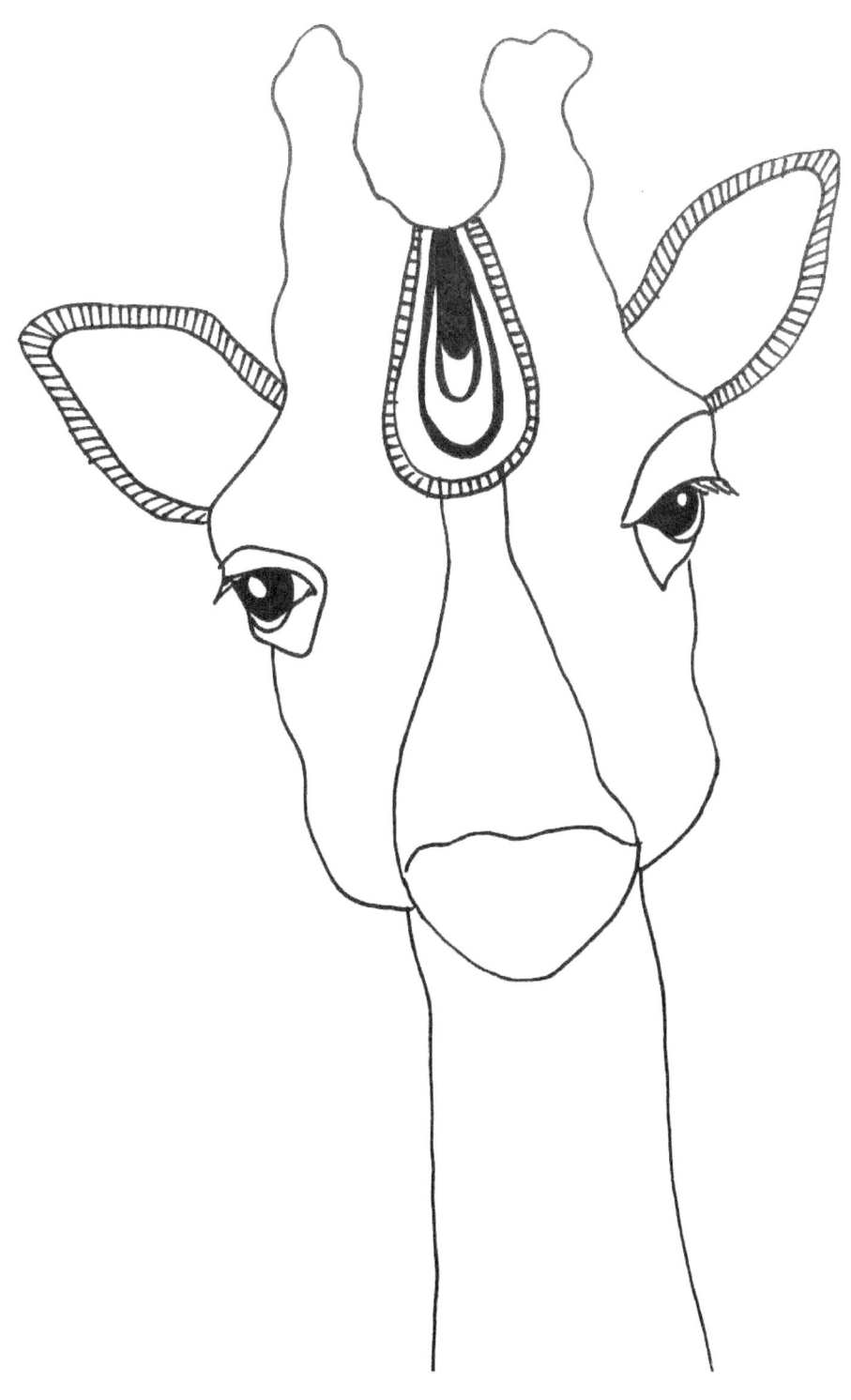

Step two: Let's do the first decorations to the ears - following the outlines draw a parallel line in each, with vertical smaller ones in the space between. Move to the forehead, to make what it is seen in the picture we will draw a large and thin drop with double lines- with tiny strokes inside- and a peacock motive inside.

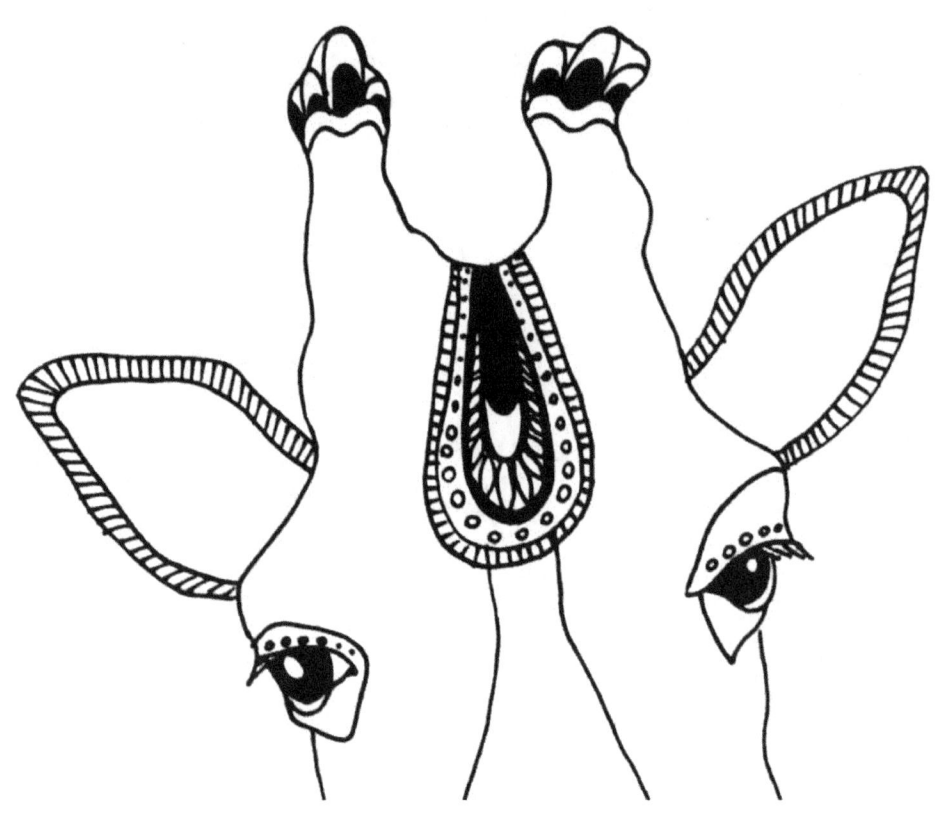

Step three: On to the horns now, draw a curvilinear line with wave shape for each, and repeat the process; above it make three arcs with smaller black arcs inside. Then move to the forehead, in the space between the drop and the peacock feather motifs, with small circles in that space, add ovals inside the peacock feather. Then pay attention to the eyes, draw various circles above the eyelashes.

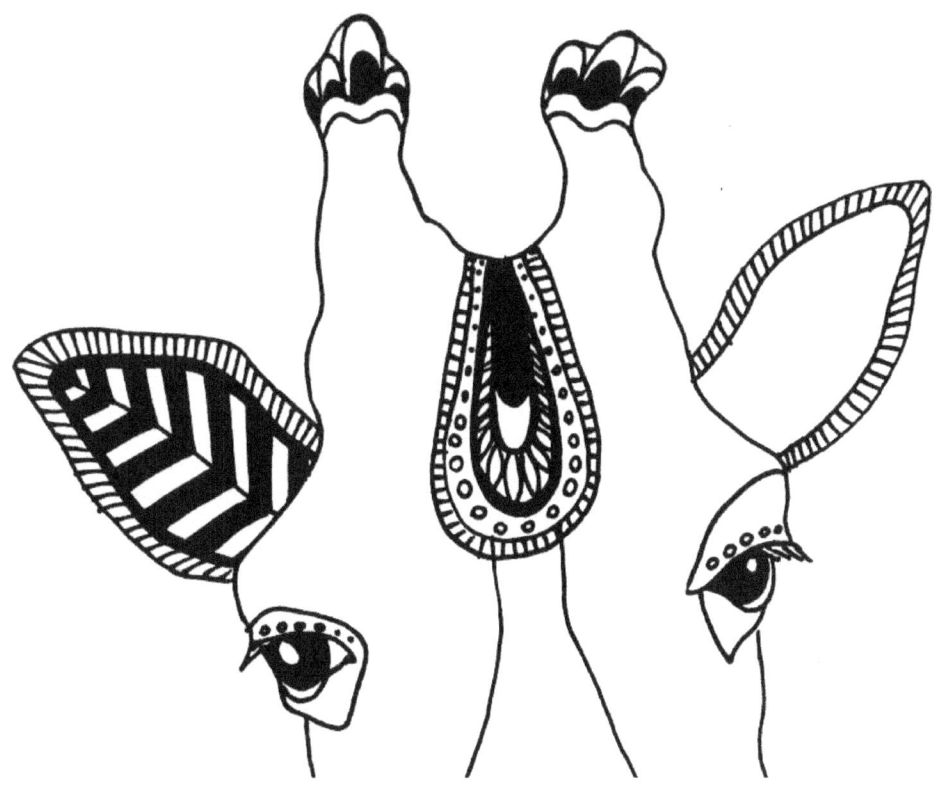

Step five: We will be working with one of the ears, this one is really easy; just draw diagonal lines encountering in the middle, with every other one being black; draw one vertical line dividing the converging lines.

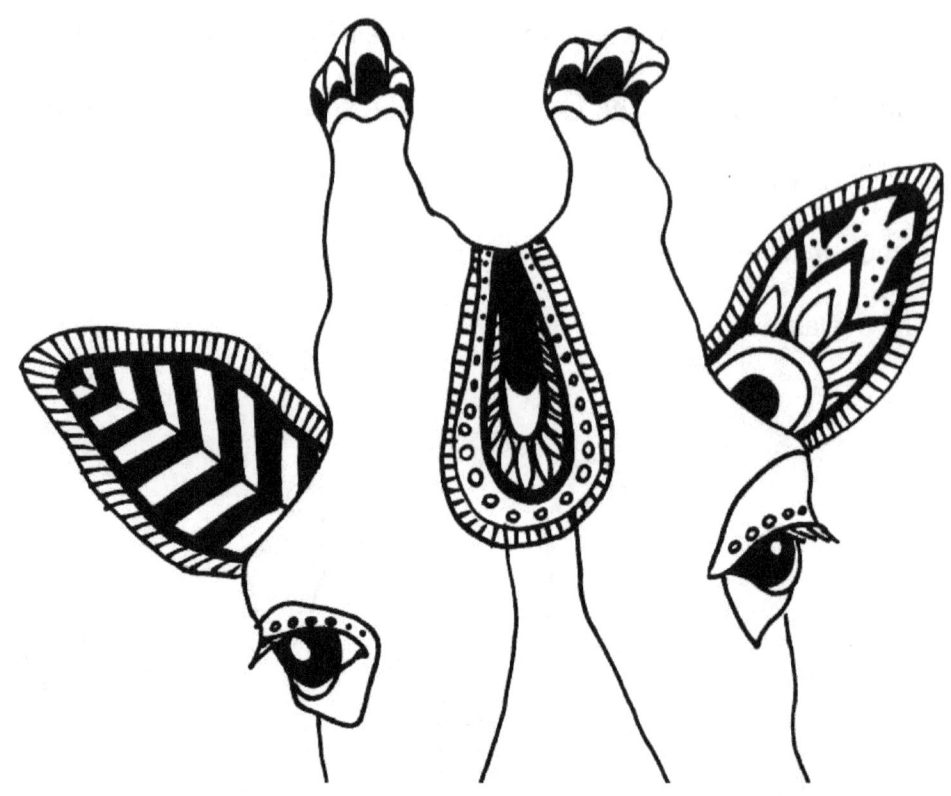

Step six: Moving to the other ear, draw a small black semicircle, with another one above that will be white, and arc just after it. Continuing from this, draw small leafs inside bigger ones with the same form, adding a broad outline to them. From the top part of the ear draw upside down black leafs, make points in the void between both figures.

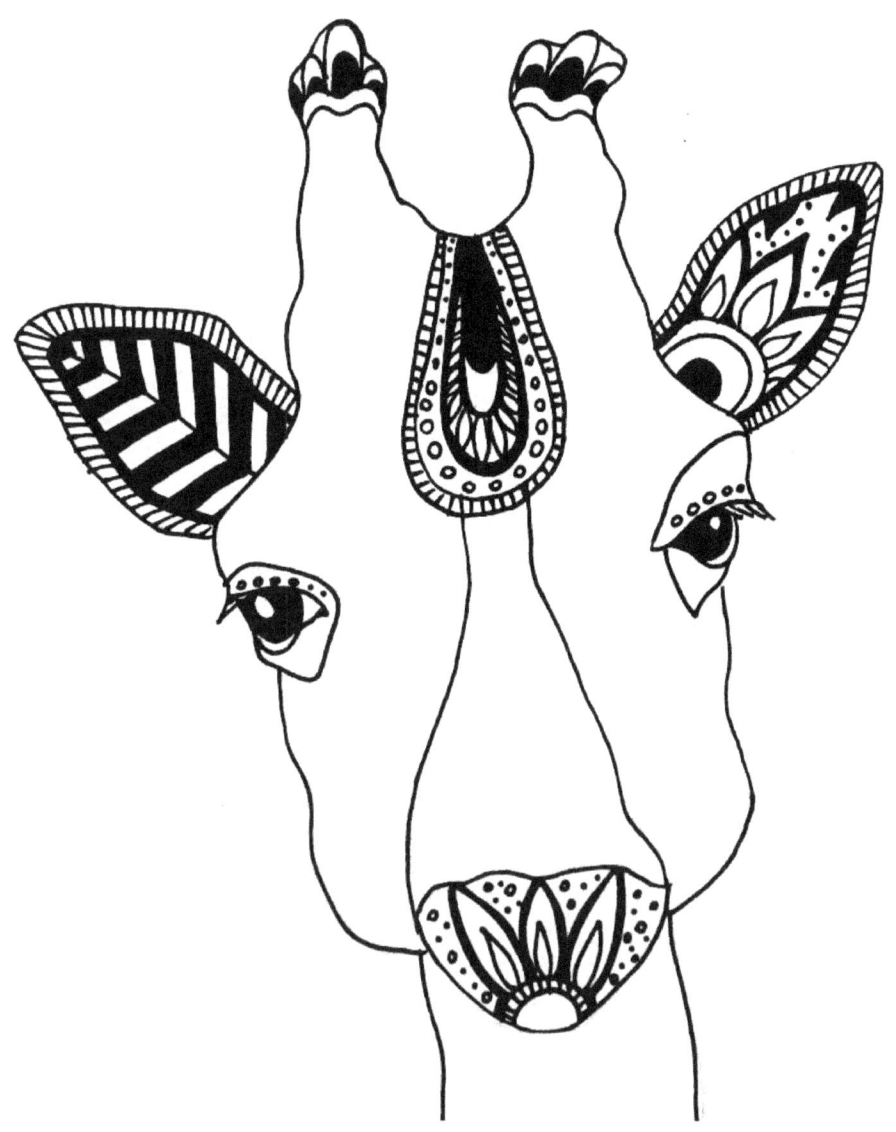

Step seven: We will work with the lower part of the nose. Make a small semicircle with a parallel one with vertical lines in between. Sketch three small petal like figures, inside bigger ones with thick lines; in the remaining space draw small points, or circles.

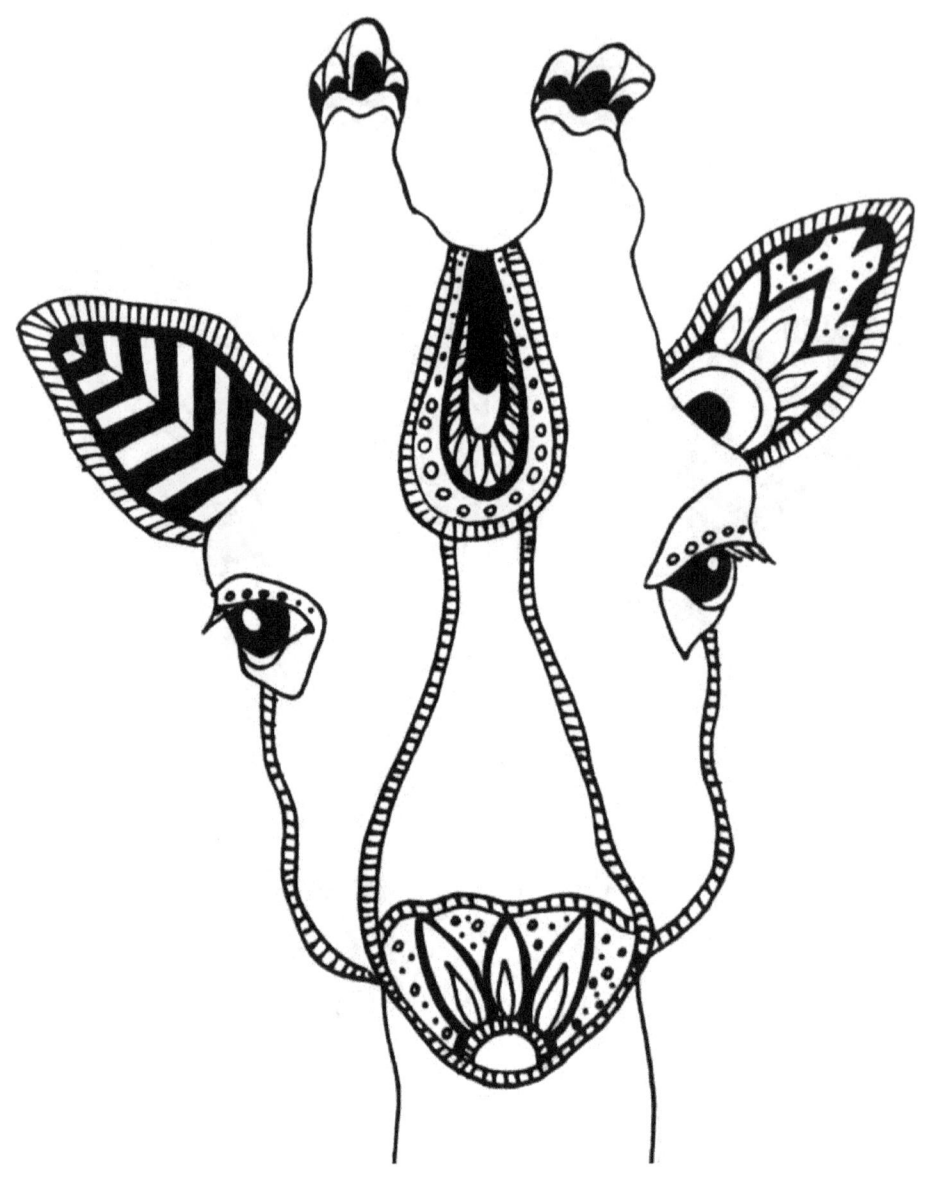

Step eight: This will be quite simple - follow the silhouette of the nose and the base of the face, from the bottom to the eyes. Make smaller lines in the space created.

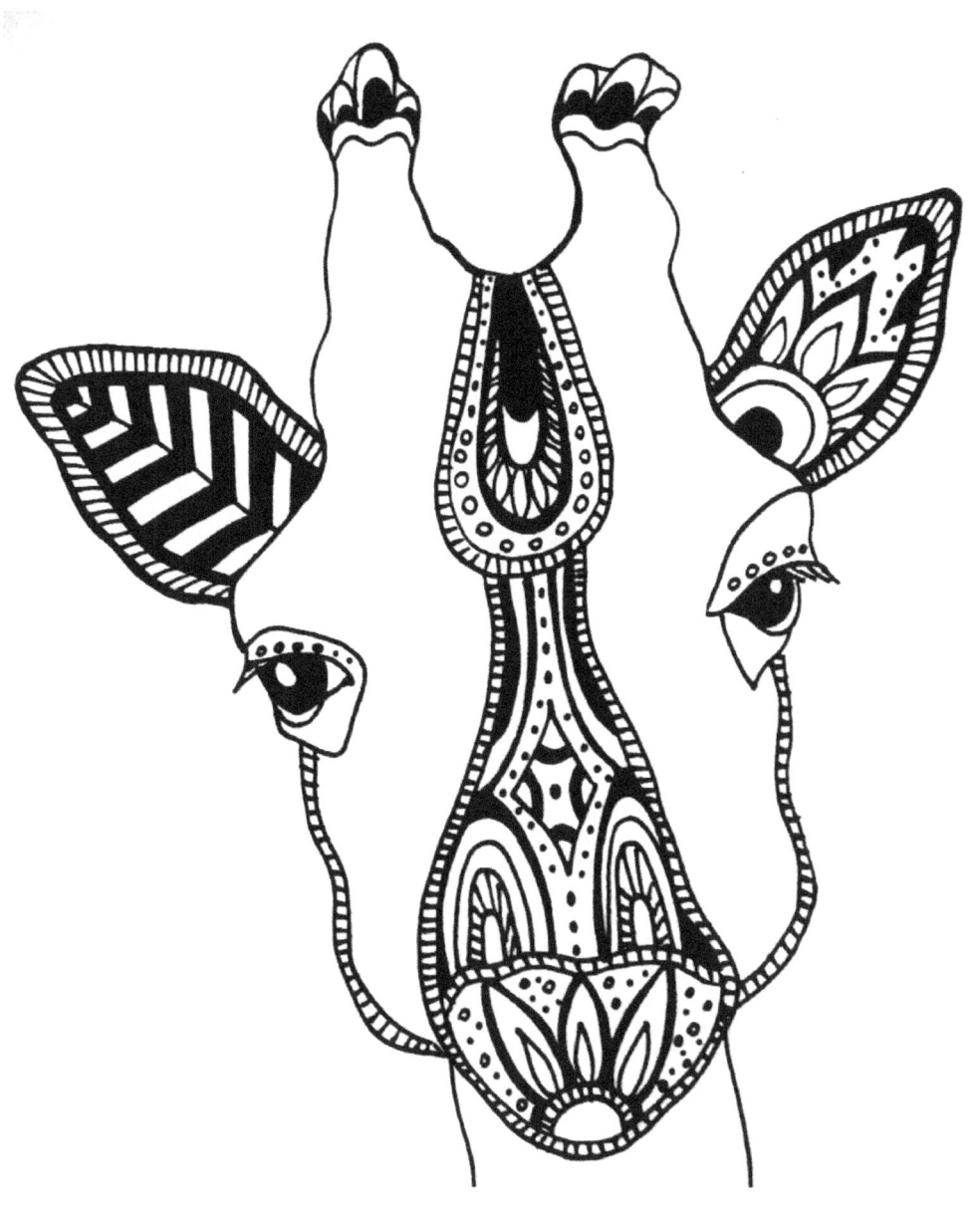

Step nine: We will work with the truncated triangle of the nose now. In the upper middle part draw a diamond that will have a black dot on the center and thick lined semicircles surrounding it. Respecting the outline of the rhombus four other large lines will be drawn around it. In the case of the section above they will have parallel lines leaving a space between them; the shape that will be formed should be painted black.

Now moving to the bottom - sketch two semicircles with a thick line outlining them; inside of this draw other three arcs, with smaller vertical lines between the last two.

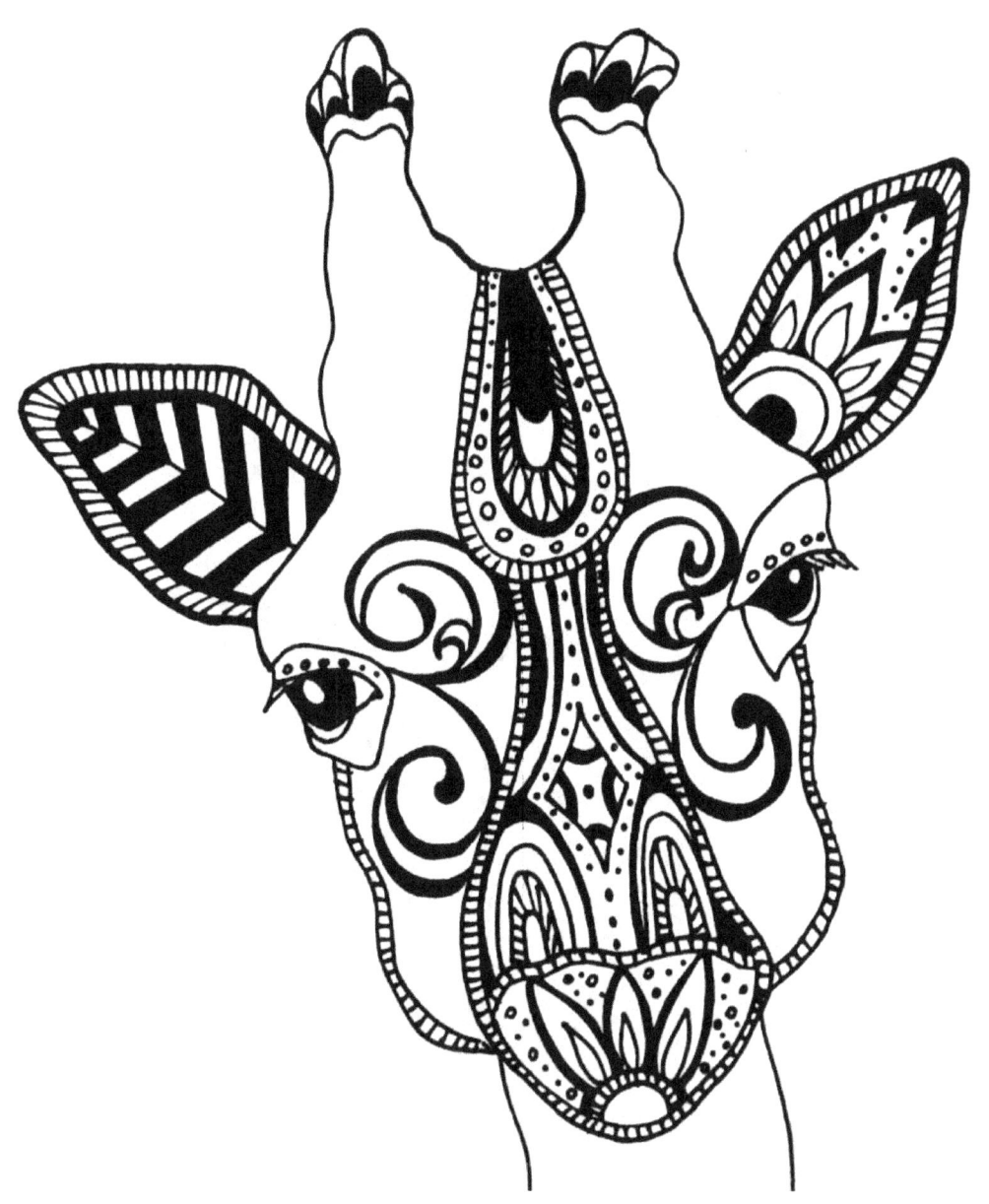

Step ten: We will work from the eyes in direction to the nose; draw thick

curls with double lines.

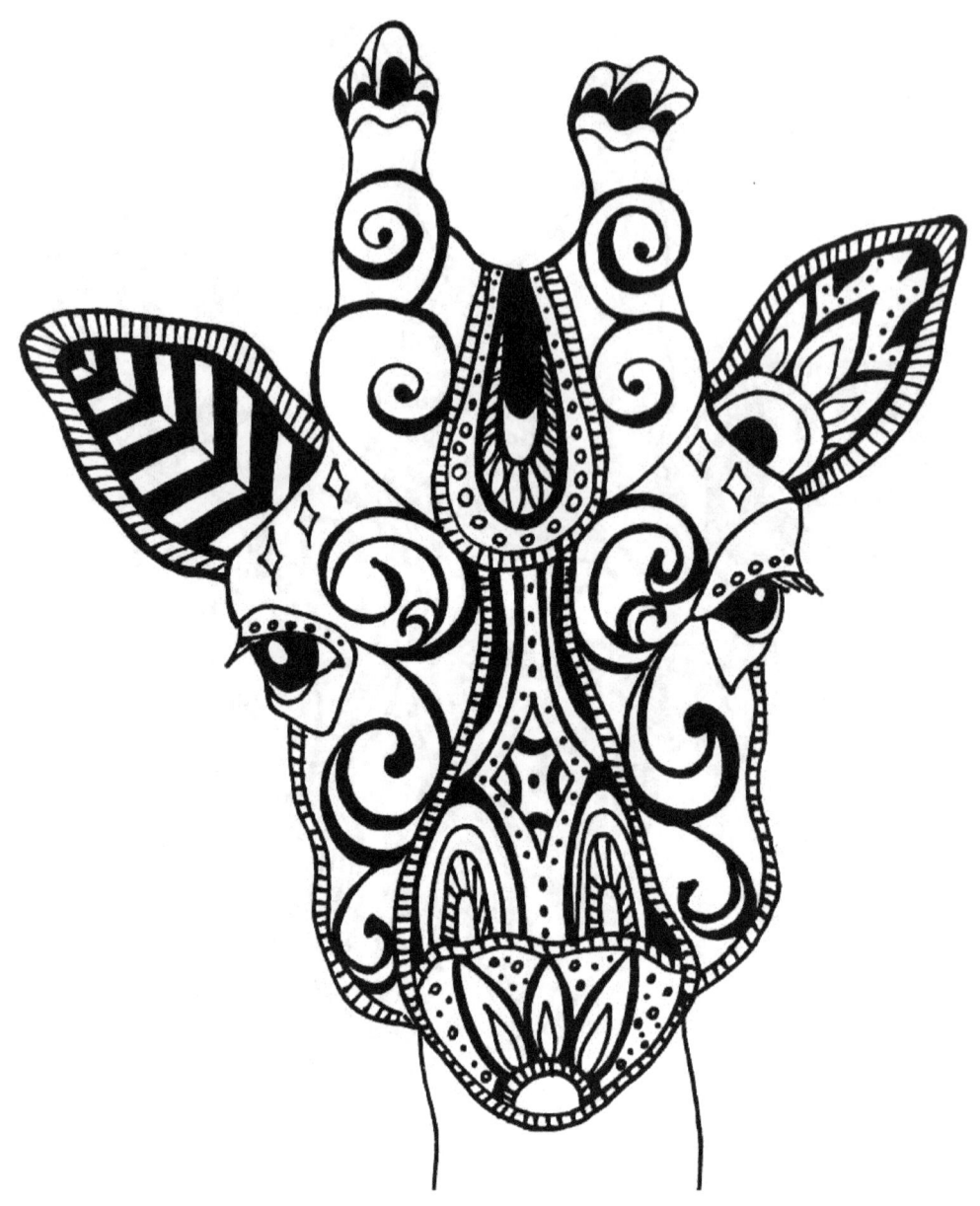

Step eleven: Draw three diamonds in diagonal at one side of the face, just

down the ear; do the same with the other ear, just look at the picture below.

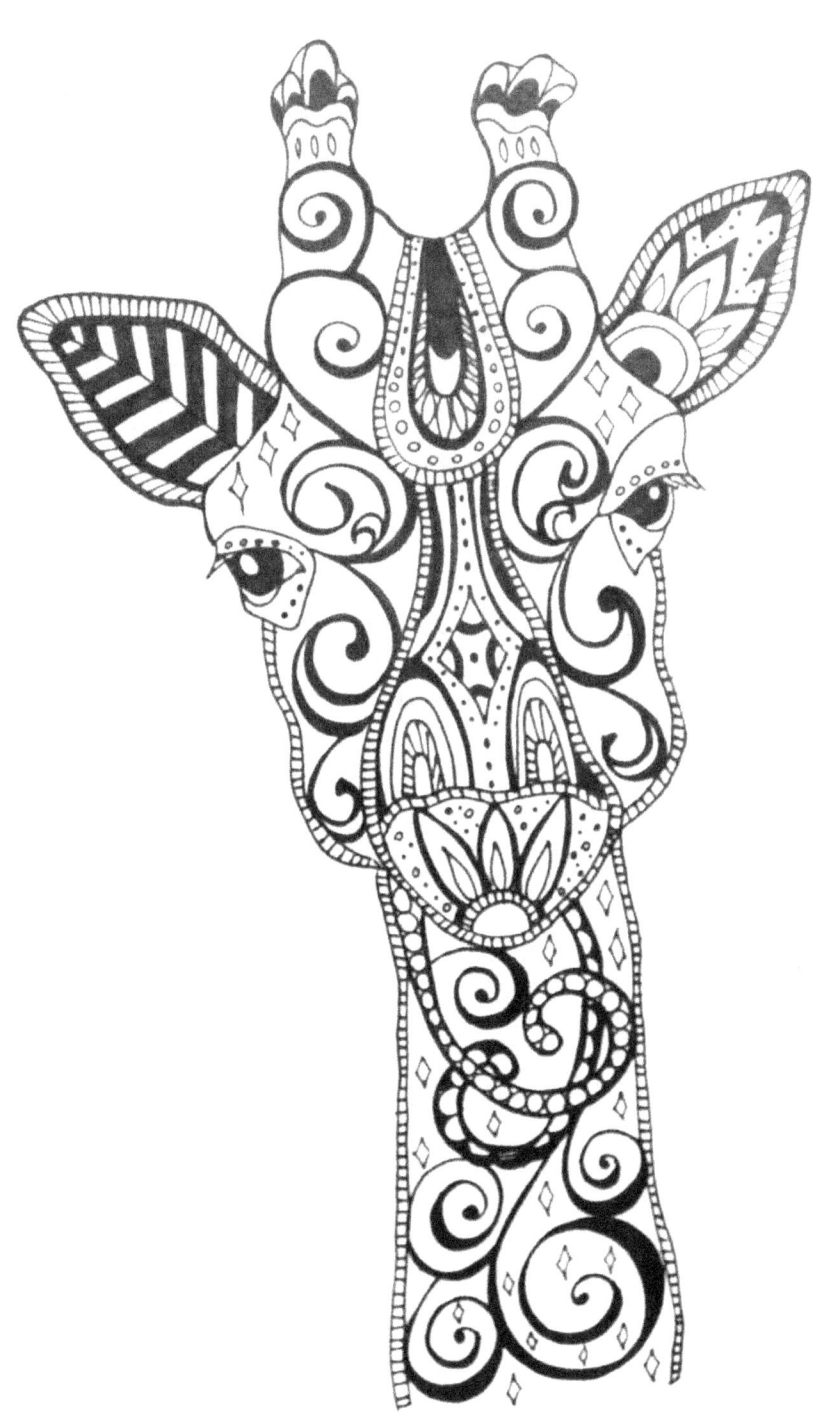

Step twelve: Now we will be focusing on the forehead; draw big thick curls on each side - the first ones making a heart shape between them, and the other ones will be on opposite directions.

In the neck the curly motive is repeated, using the thick line to draw them, with two exceptions shown above, being those two curls with circles inside of them.

The space that is left free can be occupied with rhombuses. Then, draw a parallel line to both sides of the neck and add horizontal lines in the space between.

Drawing level 3: Is that a lioness?

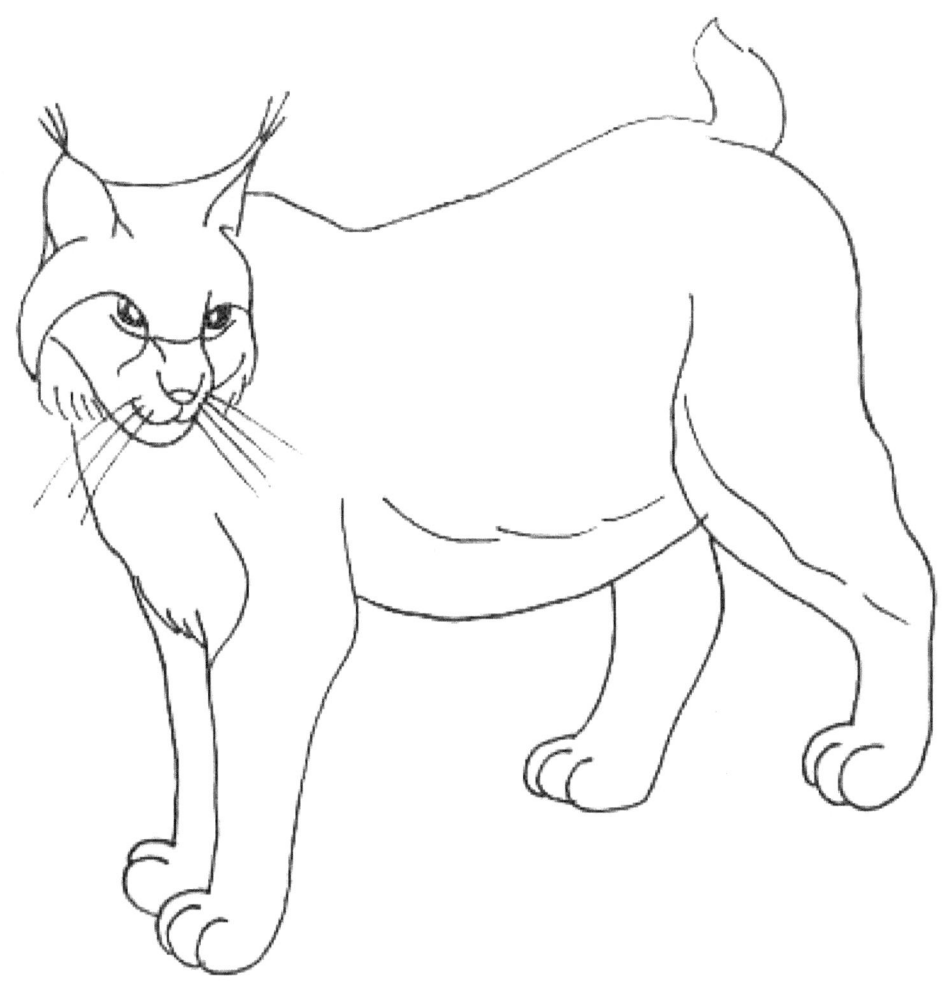

Step one: general shape.

Draw one big ellipsis in a horizontal direction for the body, and another one vertically for the visible thigh of the back legs. Then moving to the front part of the animal, you can use a vertical ellipsis again; sketch an upside down hexagon that will serve as the base of the face. In the lower part of this figure draw seven straight lines, three to one side and the remaining ones to the other.

Small upside down arcs converging into another reversed semicircles, with another arc inside of it. The eyes will be like chestnuts; after this, both ears and the tail can be made working from the base of triangles.

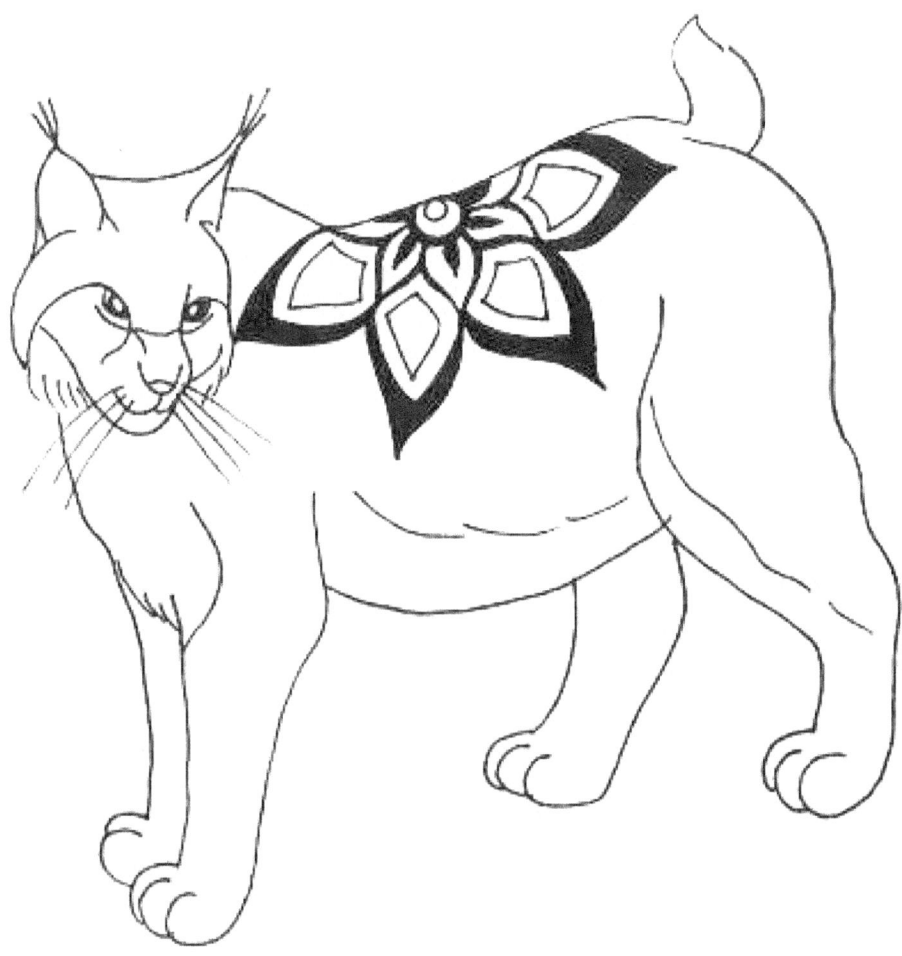

Step two: We will concentrate our efforts on the back of the creature; the figure, as it seen above is like a flower. Starting with an small circle, having another one inside, sprouting small black leafs from there, continuing from this draw parallel figures to those just described; between two set of petals draw a thick penciled triangle, repeat this four times. Then make a small shield like form inside of them.

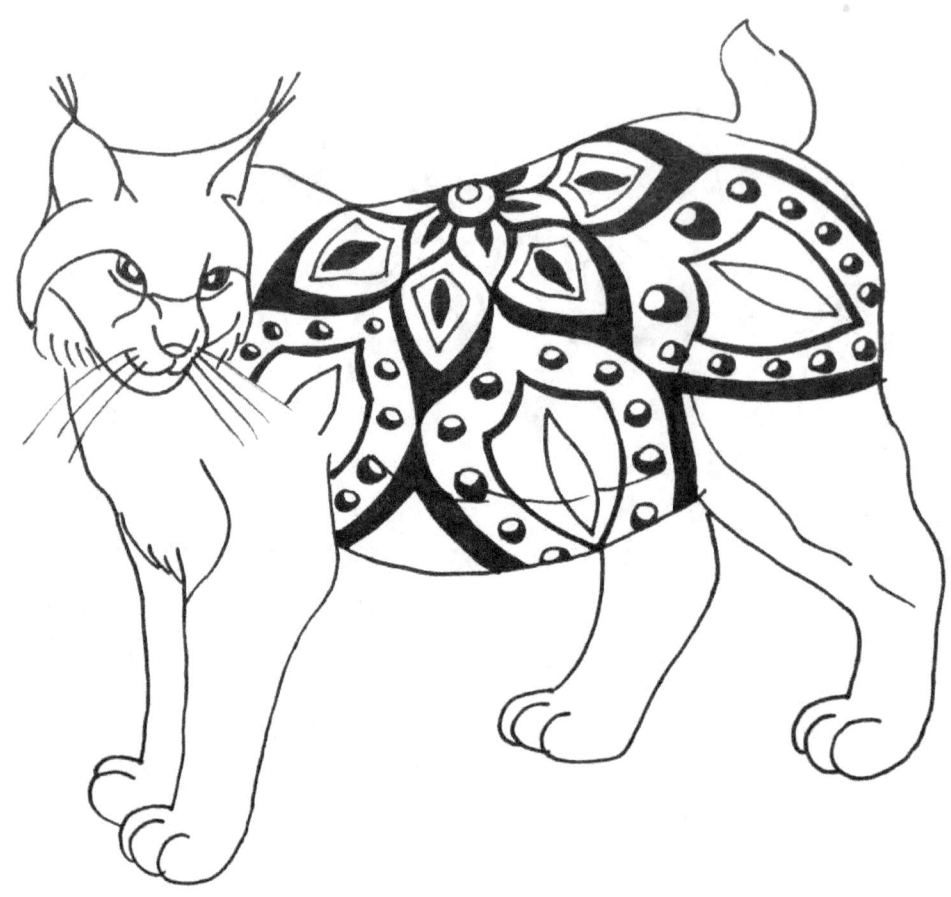

Step three: Continuing with the shields we will draw leaf like black figures inside them. Moving on from beside of the front leg to the thigh we will be sketching with thick lines three shields like figures, with black and white figure inside of them, and another shield with a thinner line and another vertical leafs inside.

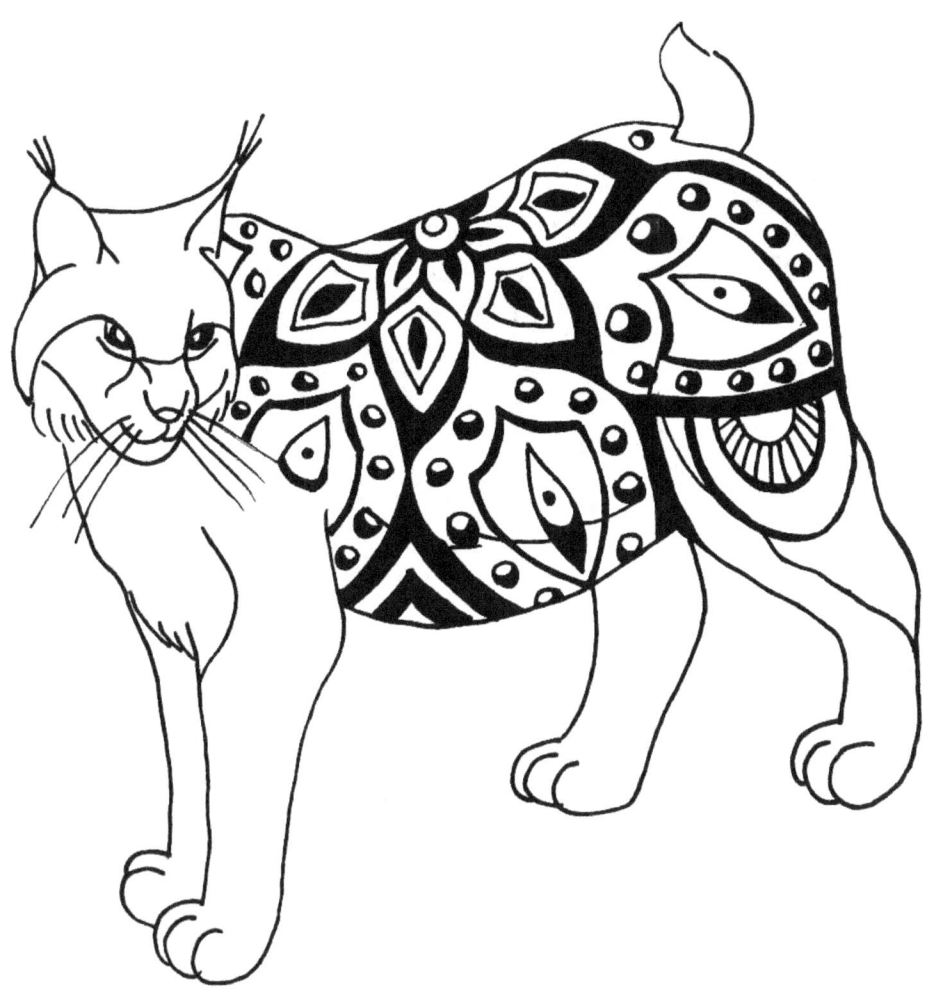

Step four: Let's move to the back visible leg, below the shield make a reverse semicircle, then another one further separated, sketch vertical lines in the void that is left, after that make another arc; to complete this draw a diagonal line across the thigh.

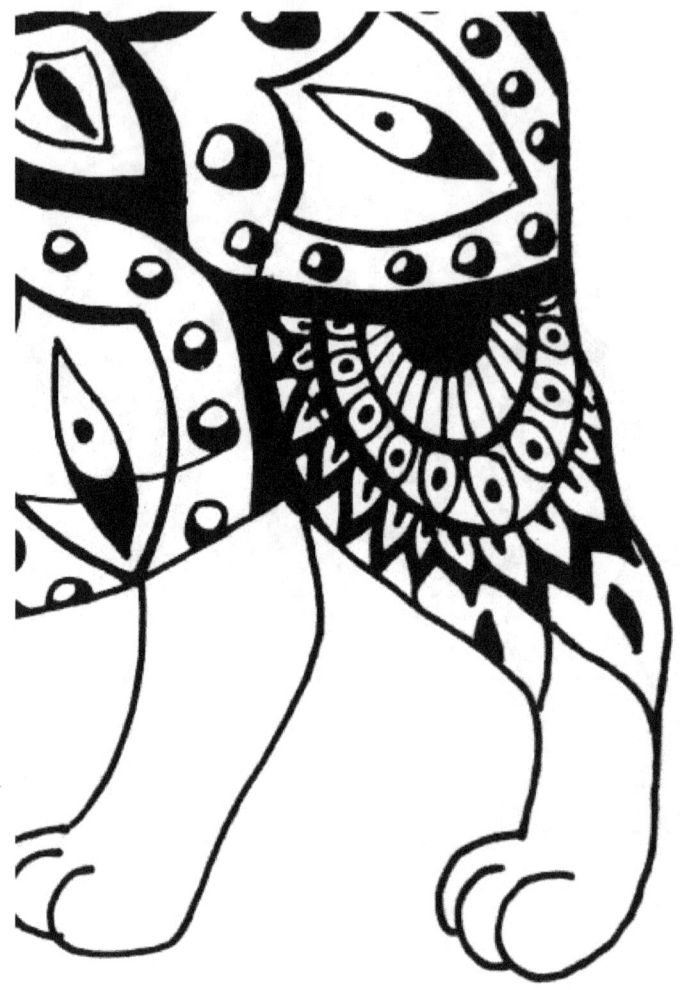

Step five: Continuing on the back limb, we will be adding small ovals in the space between the semicircle and the arc-this ovals will have black dots inside of them; small black triangles will be drawn surrounding the arc, engulfing them we will make various thick petals; finally two curve lines will serve to separate the thigh from the leg, the space remaining will be fill with two strokes.

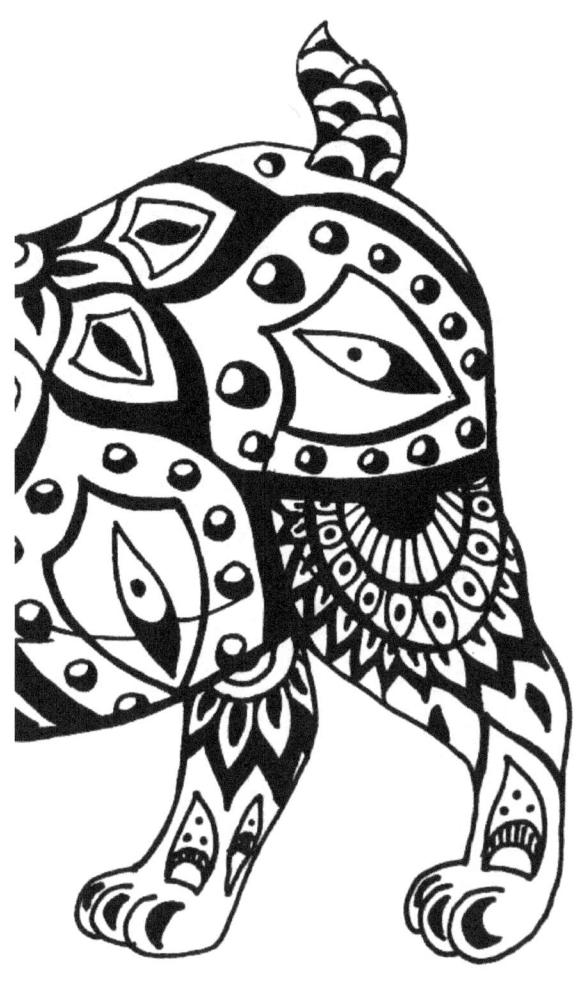

Step six: Continuing on the back limbs, and still working with the same leg, draw two curved lines with small points and semicircle inside; this figure will be accompanied by two arcs separated by various vertical lines. Jump to the other leg beside it, repeat the same process, and make a petal like form that will have two arcs with vertical lines inside. Moving onto the claws, to draw them create three crescent black moon on each paw.

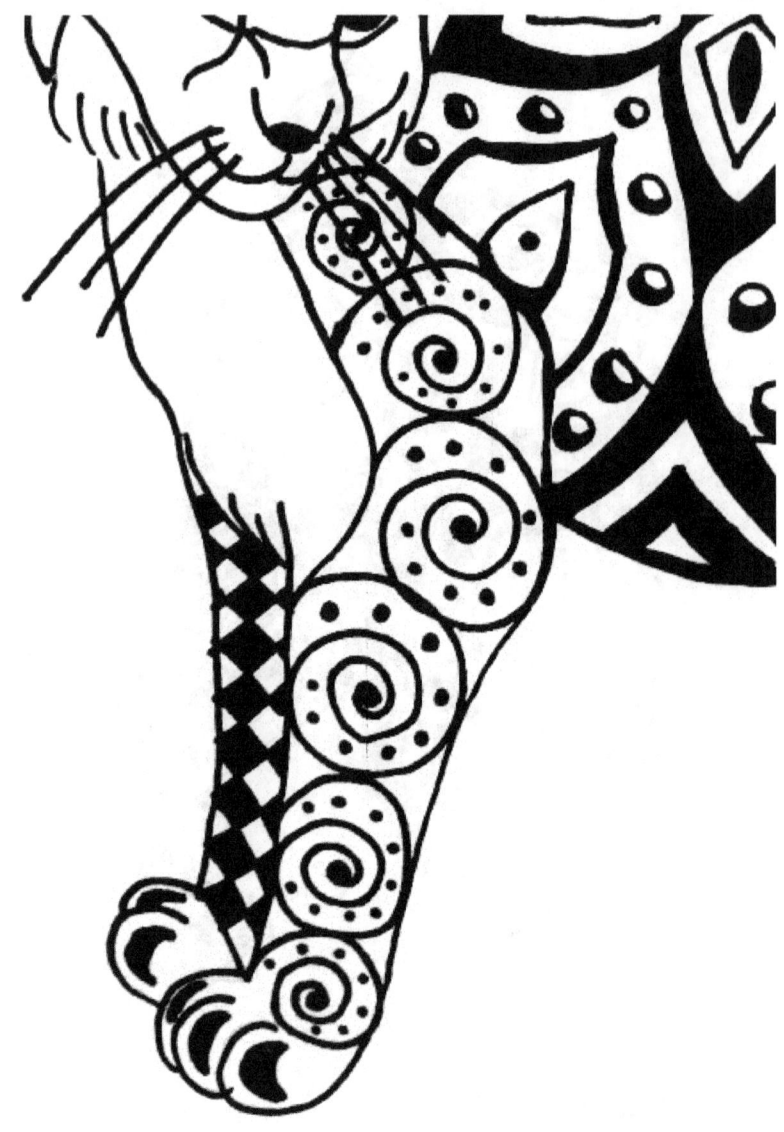

Step seven: You will be depicting various spirals with dots inside of them - on the leg nearer to us. For the limb next to it draw black and white diamonds. Finally repeat the crescent black moons for the claws on both paws.

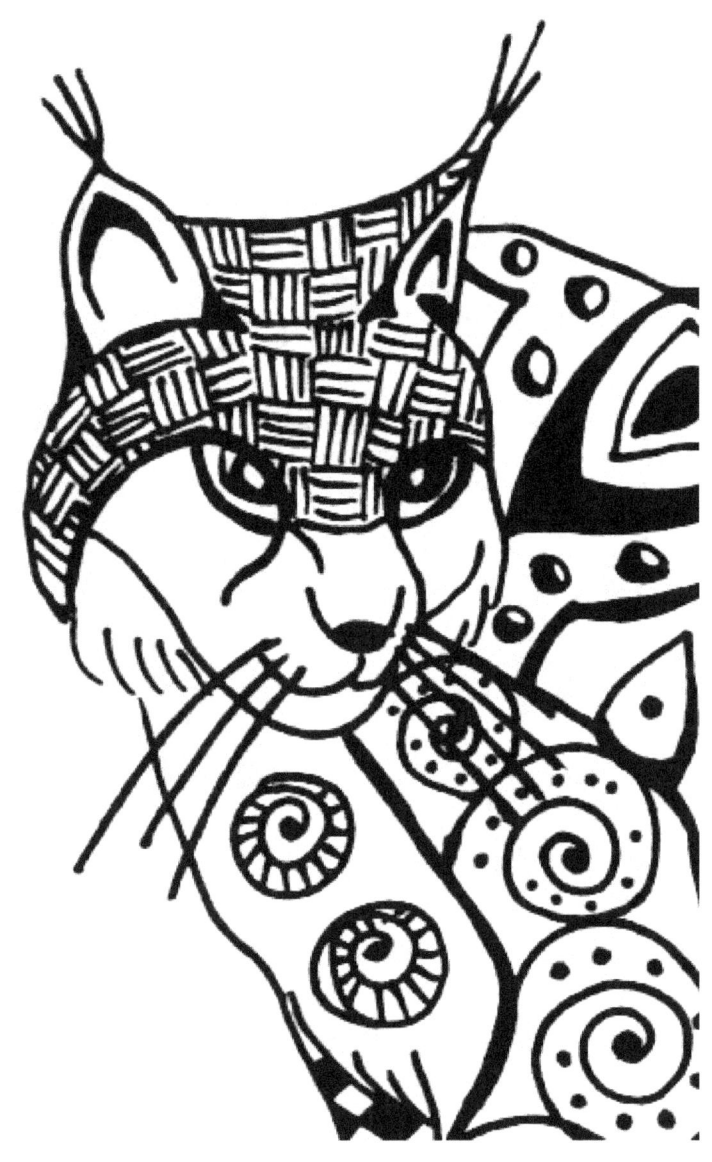

Step eight: Draw two shells like spirals in a diagonal on the chest of the beast. After this, work on the top part of the head, from the eyes to the ears draw a wicker like basket texture.

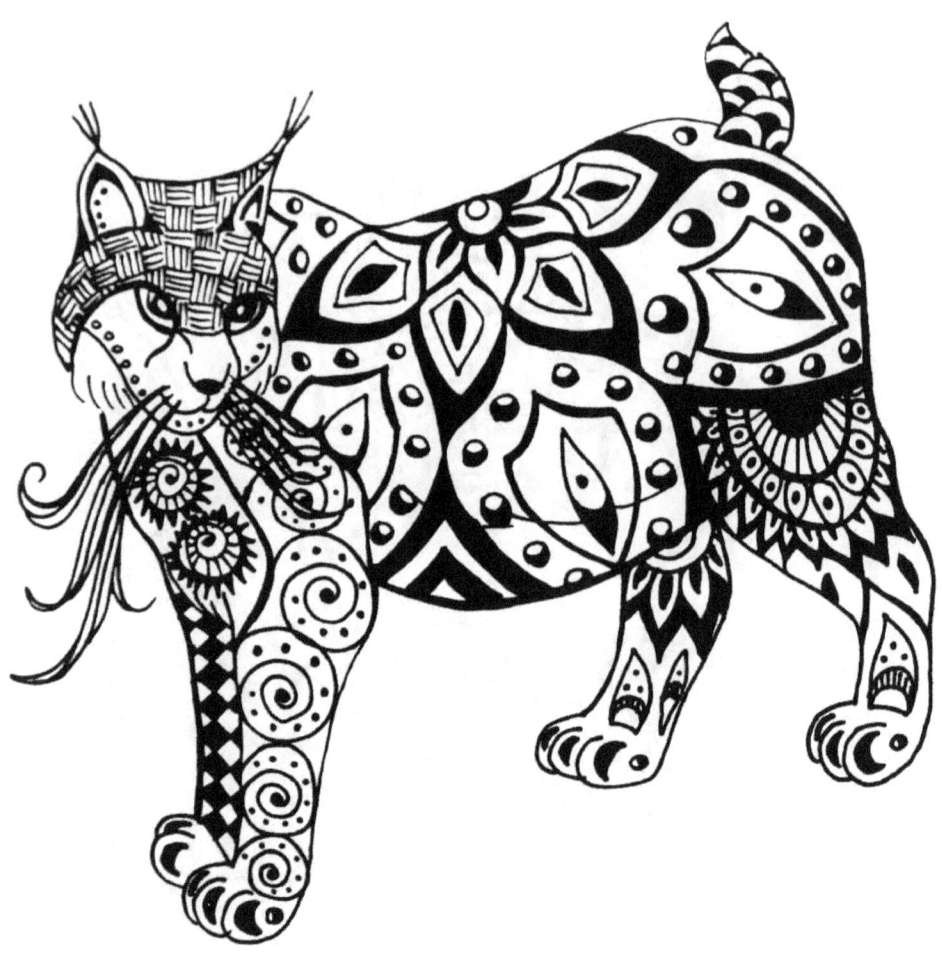

Step ten: Let's start with the finishing touches now; draw small dots with black and white on the paws. Add various triangles to the figures on the creature chest. To the whiskers add various long and curled irregular lines. Sketch blank dots for the jaws; put an arc inside each ear with dots inside one of them. Move to the tail - draw black semicircles and white arcs. There you will have this lioness complete.

Drawing level 4: The growling panther

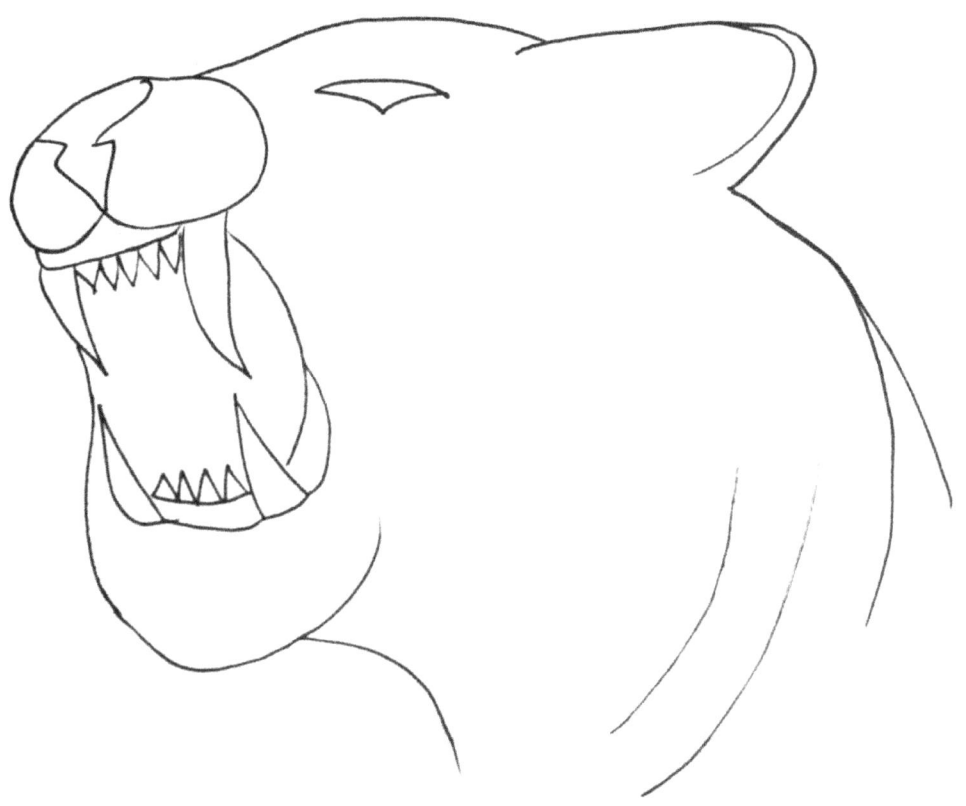

Step one: general form.

Let's sketch the lines for the animal head as it is seen from a profile; the forehead will be formed by a curved line, and then two arcs will make the ear. Cracked lines will continue the head, and large curved lines will be to show the neck; the outline for the neck will be an arc. Another arc will serve for the jaw. Inside the gaping mouth draw various triangles that will be serve as pointy teeth; to draw the side of the mouth we will use an arc. Use two huge circles for the nose with an upside down triangle and an oval in the center. The eye will be drawn with a small triangle with curved vertices.

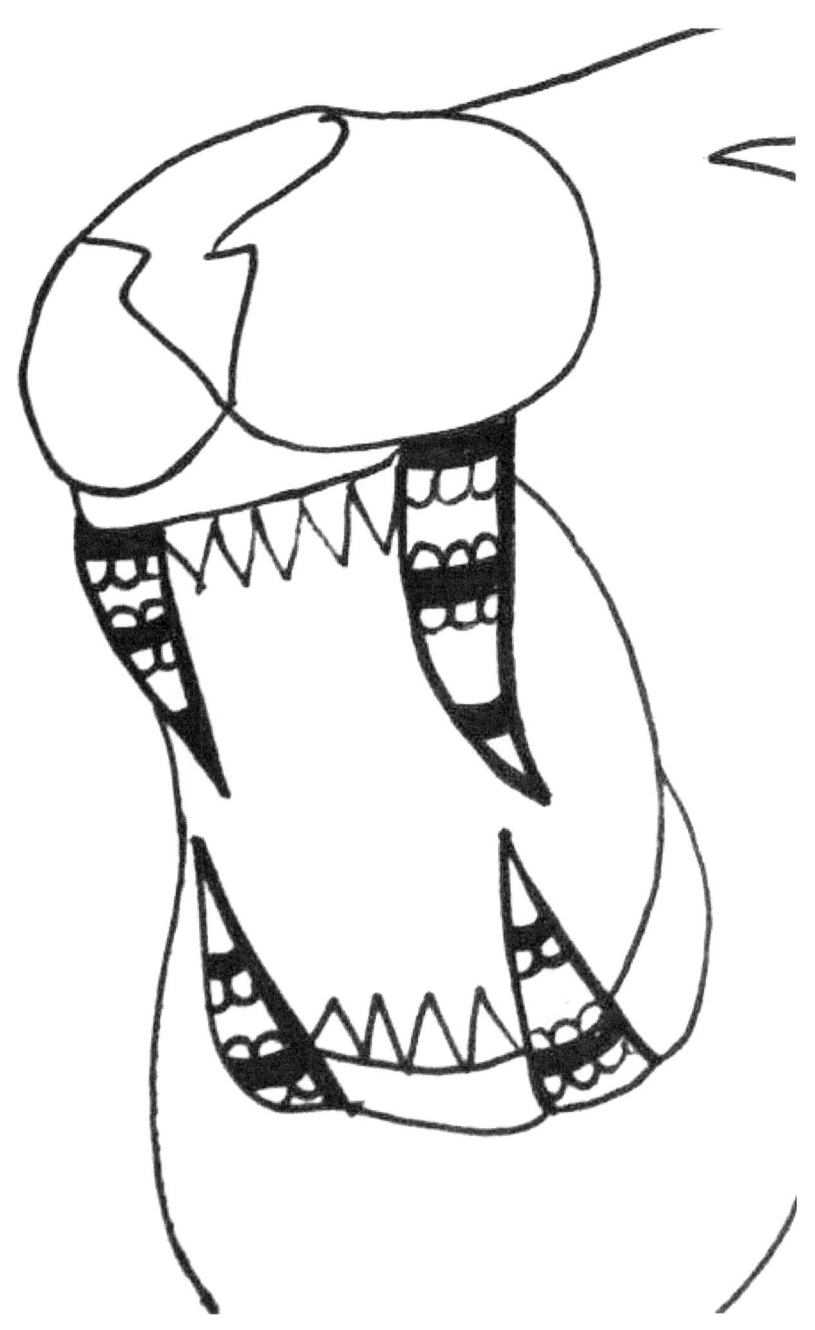

Step two: We will focus on the fangs - for the four of them we will be working with broad black horizontal lines, some of them will be accompanied by small semicircles.

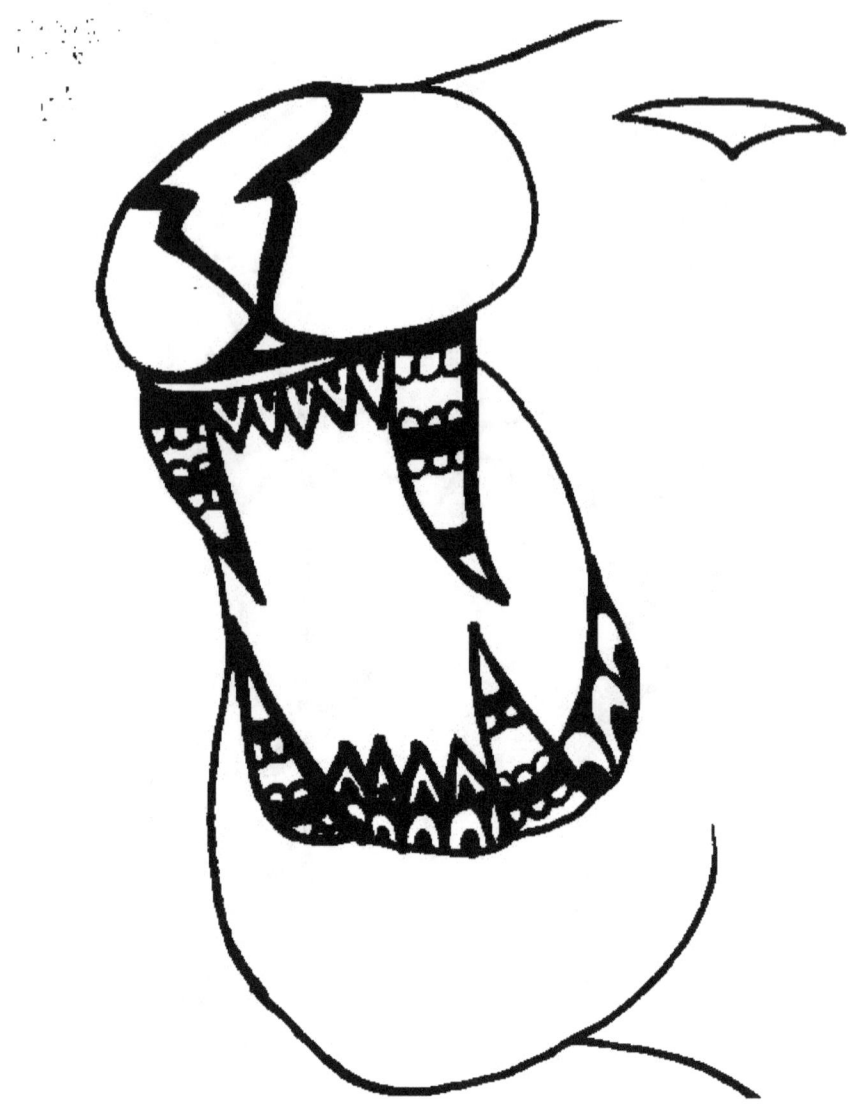

Step three: For the teeth we will make thicker lines and add small black triangles; on the lower jaw we also will sketch arcs and semicircles. On the nose we will outline the upside triangle and oval with a broad line.

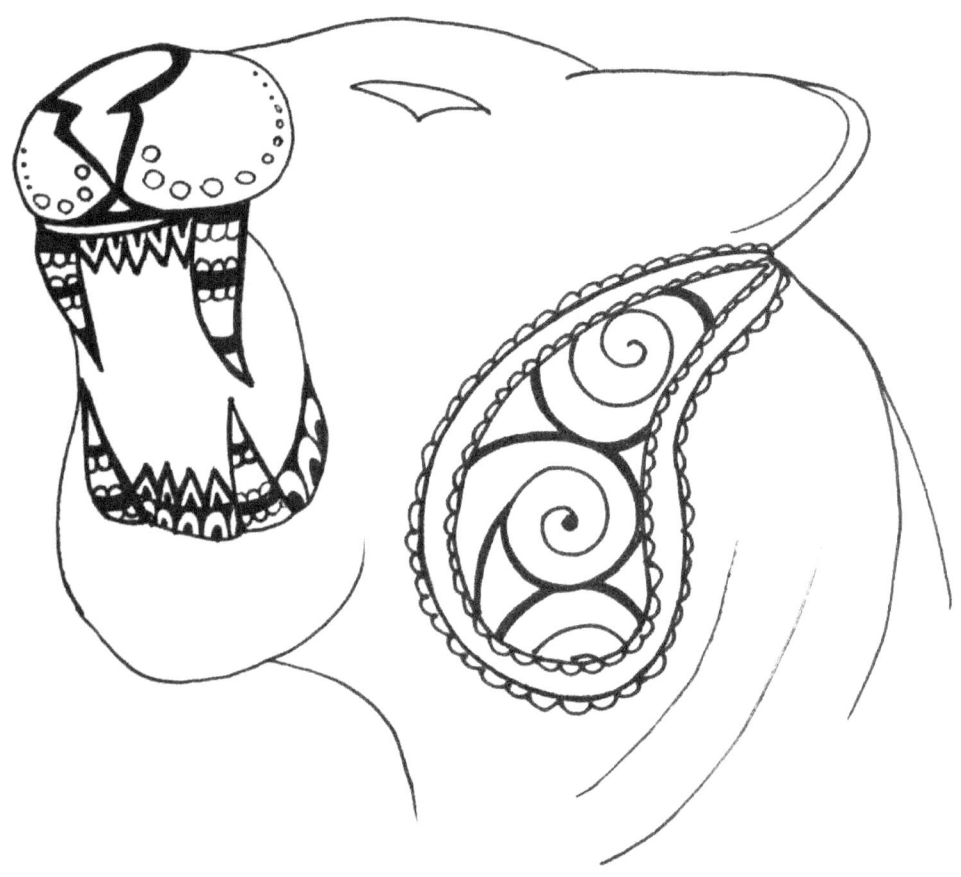

Step four: Draw various white dots on the nose of the beast. Move to the neck and draw a huge drop, and inside of it - another one; on the outline of both draw various arcs. On the interior we will draw three spirals, with thicker outlines.

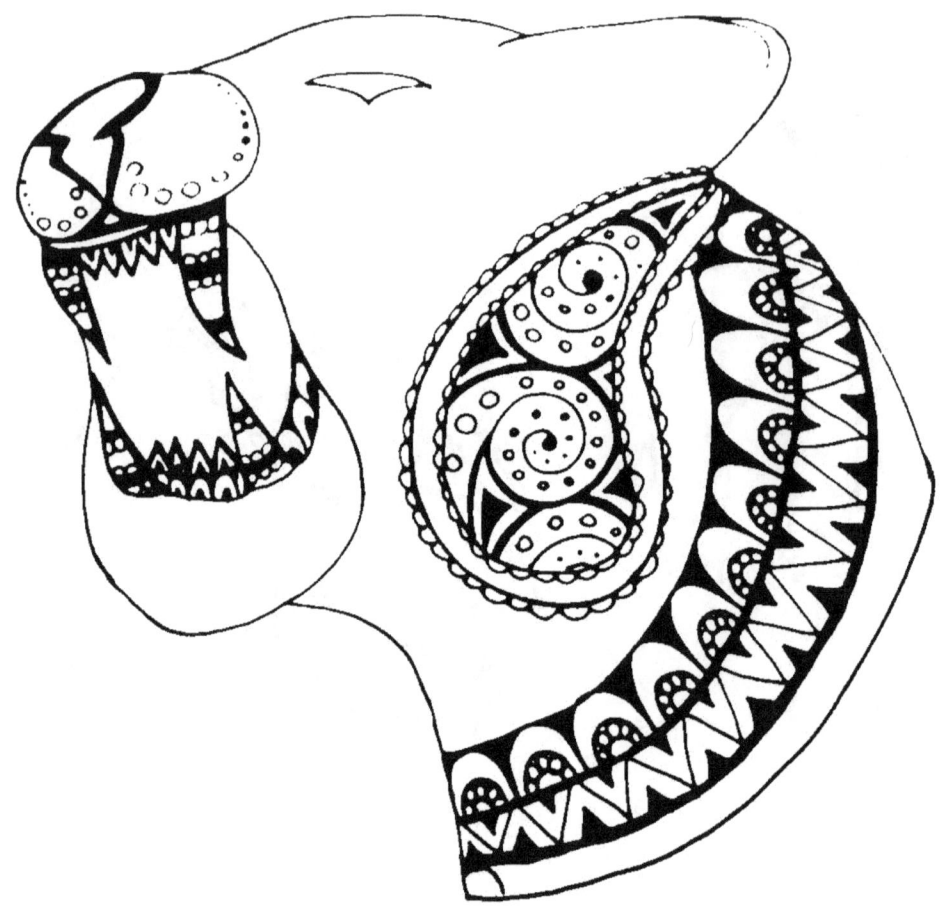

Step five: Add some white dots inside the spirals; draw black triangles on the space in between this figures. Draw a sort of curved paper wallie, use various arcs one right after the other, with small semicircles inside, that will also have small circles in them. A thick line parallel to the last one will divide this from various upside down white triangles with smaller black ones inside them, then regular triangles with the same design will be just below, and after that a broad black line.

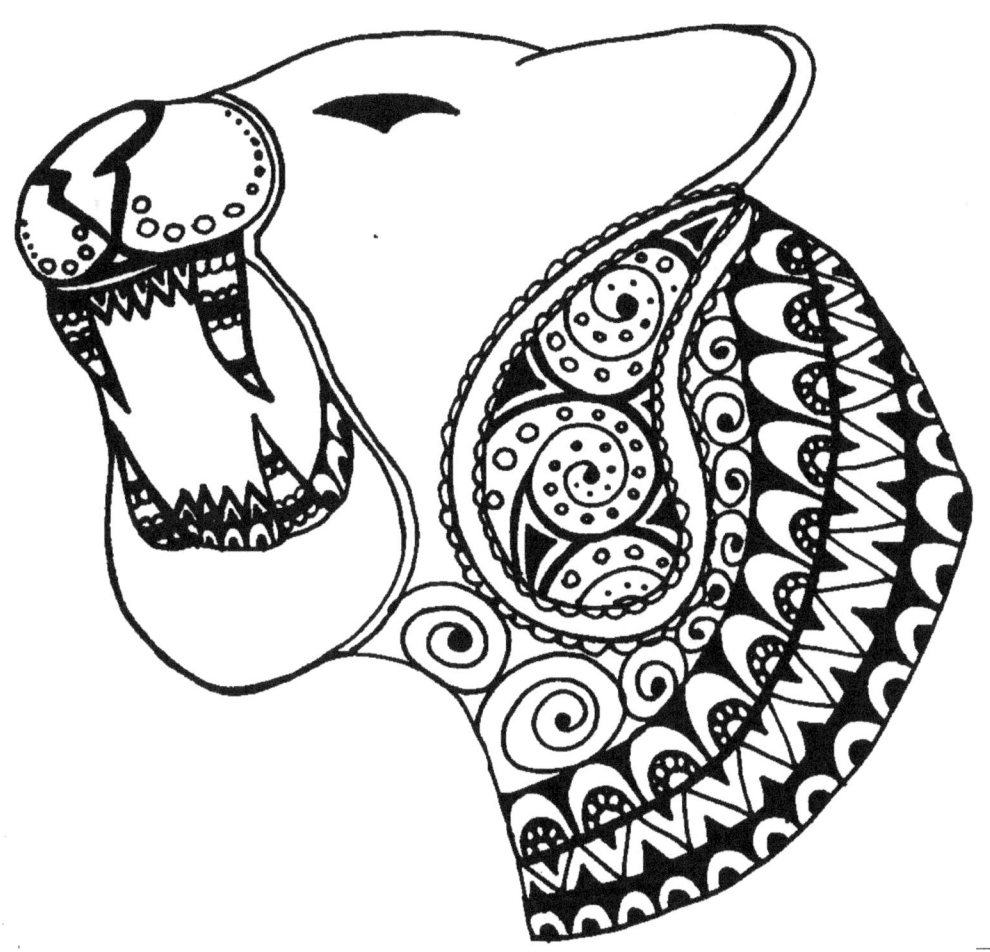

Step six: Paint the eye black. On the space between the curved motive and the drop motive make various spirals.

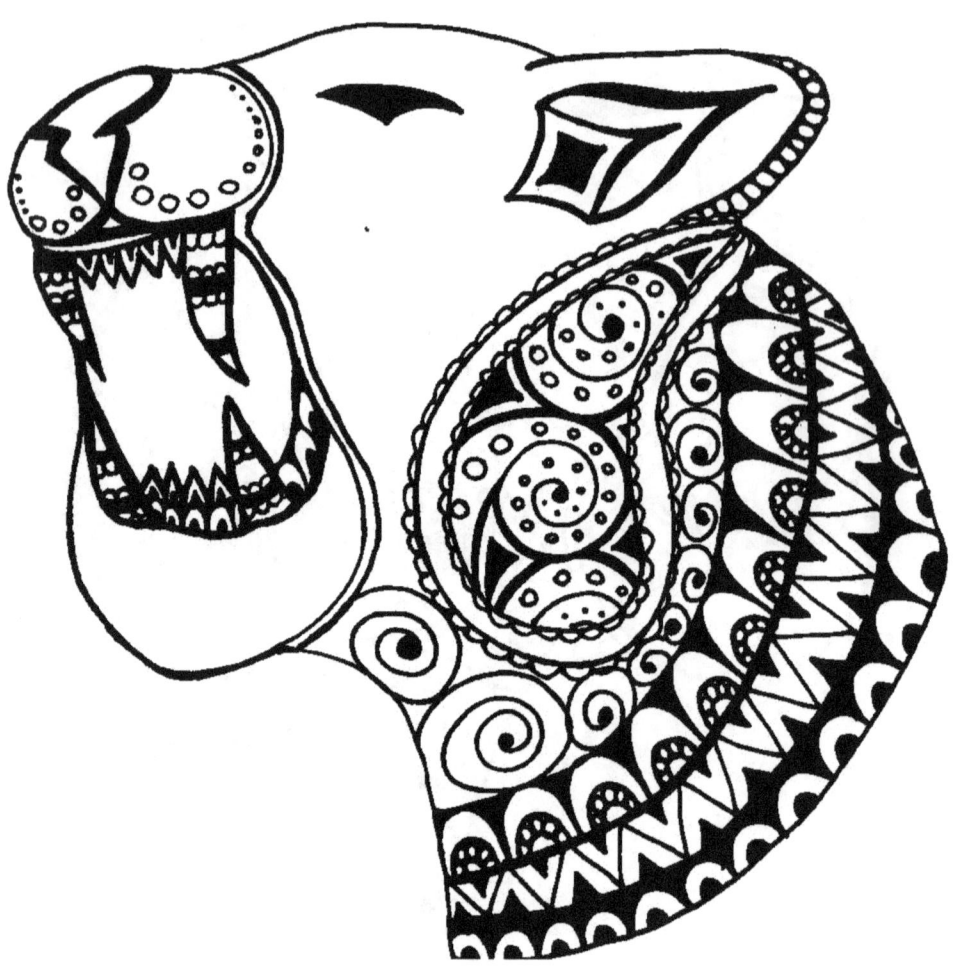

Step seven: Draw various white dots following the silhouette of the ear. Sketch a diamond with another one smaller, and this time black inside; make thick curved lines looking like a drop. Sketch the contour of the jaw to the nose.

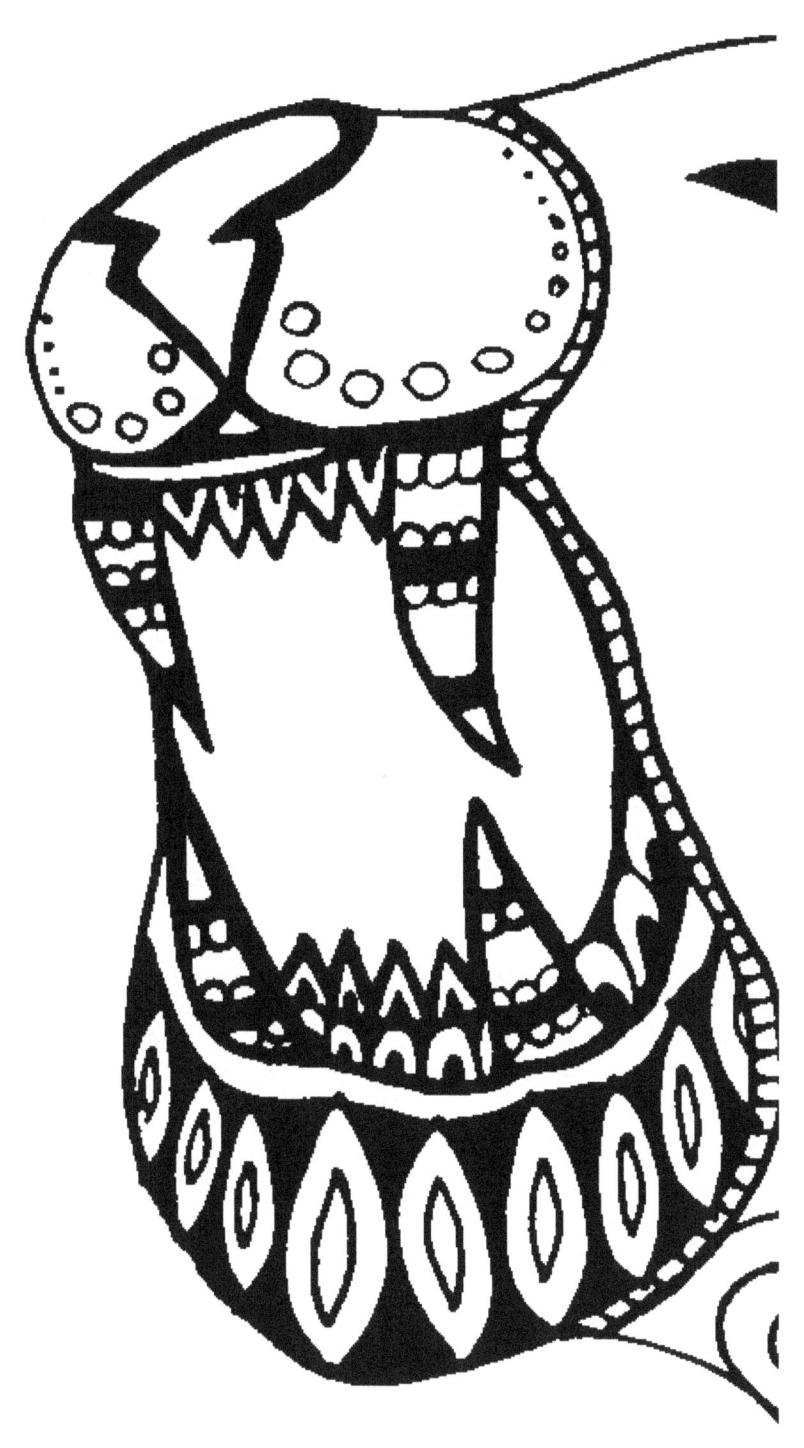

Step eight: We will add thicker lines to the teeth and fangs. Draw horizontal lines right one next to the other. Various vertical leafs with smaller leaves inside will be drawn on the jaw; both of them are white with black background.

Step nine: Paint the space between the spirals black.

Draw black semicircles inside bigger empty ones, it will look like flakes. Make similar lines to that of the eyes. Draw in the ears various circles with small black dots inside. On the top the head we will draw spirals.

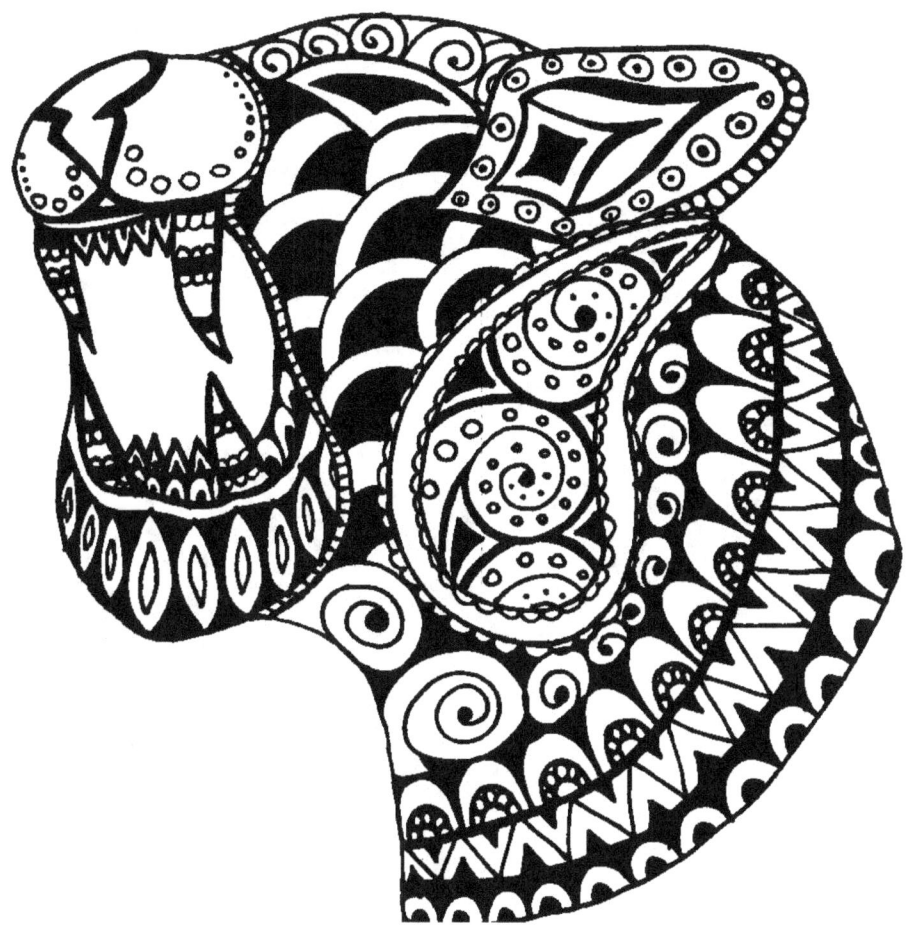

Step ten: Sketch various curved lines inside the creature mouth, and then draw zigzag lines inside each of them. There you will have your panther.

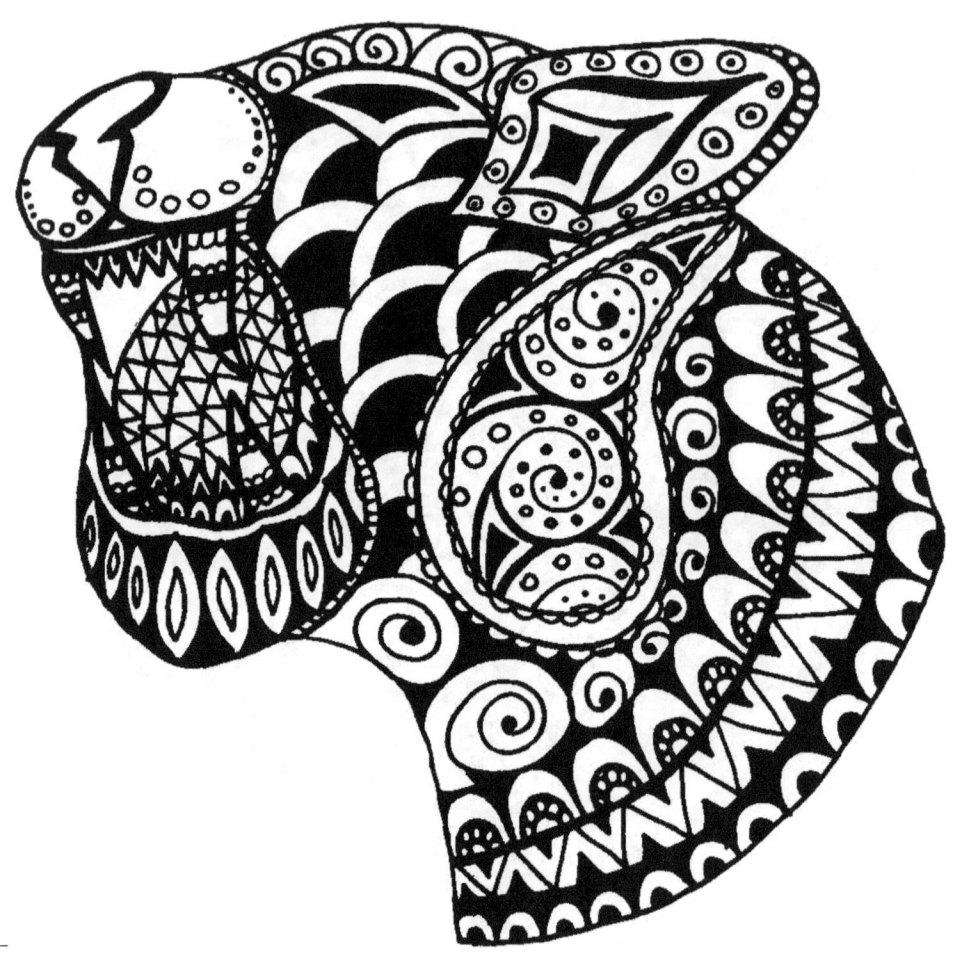

Drawing level 5: One tiger gazes

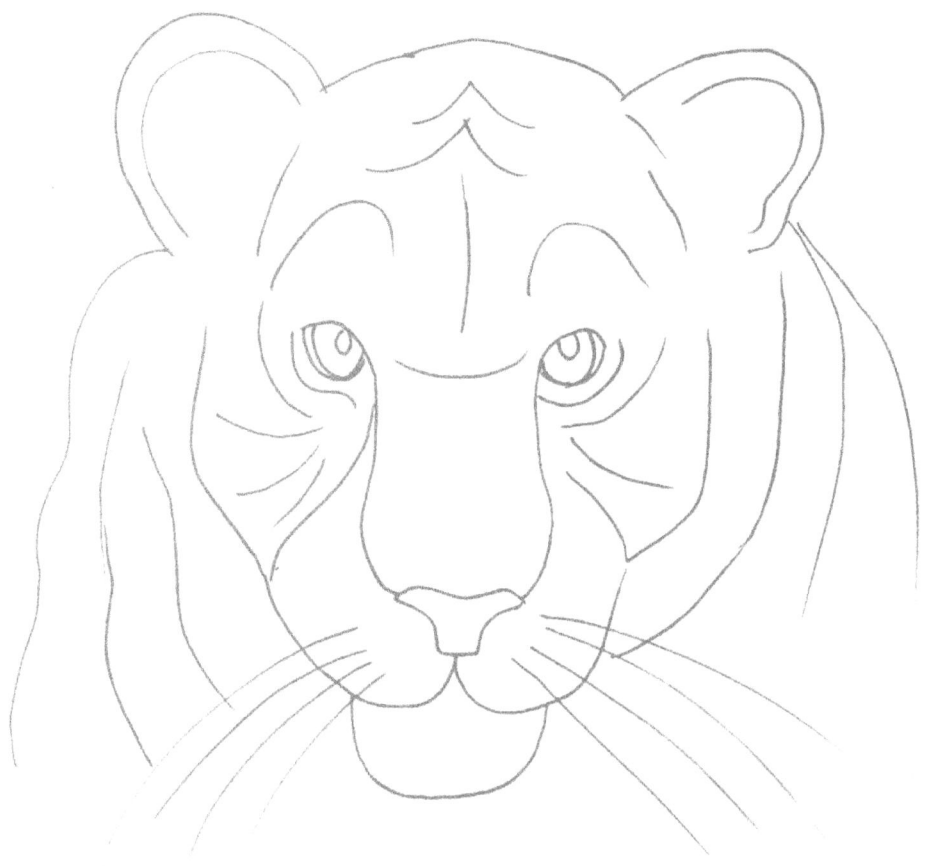

Step one: Now we will be starting with a tiger from the front. For the upper part of the head draw a long arc, to the sides draw one arc inside a smaller one. For the forehead make four consecutive "v"; then add a vertical line, and just below it a horizontal slightly curved one (this will be the middle of the beast face). To make this easier you could repeat the process of one side on the other. Let's take the right side as a reference. Just near the horizontal curved line, draw an empty chestnut shape, then inside a curved line with it lower part pointing to the center, after this make one tiny drop.

Moving on, from the eye draw one "s" shaped long vertical curved line. Keeping the eye as a reference point, make a "s" horizontal curve below it, just to the side make a vertical "c" curved, on a vertical position. Above the eye draw one arc (between this figure and the one besides the eye you will get a "c" shaped figure). Below this you will sketch three-or two if you want-lengthy curves. To the side of this make a crooked vertical arc.

Continuing from there, sketch an upside down arc, below this, make a curved line, this will work as the lower part of the mouth, the line above will work as the upper part. Between the "s" shaped curved that comes from the eye and the upside arc you will be drawing "v" in a side position. On the up part of the mouth, siding to the opposite sides draw four parallel curved lines-they will work as whiskers-.

To the sides of the crooked line make another one, like a zig-zag, make another one-almost equal, but slightly smaller and bit downwards-. Then from the outer arc of the ear make a long curved line that will be as lengthy as the distance between the ear and the down part of the mouth. Now, make the same process on the other side of the beast face.

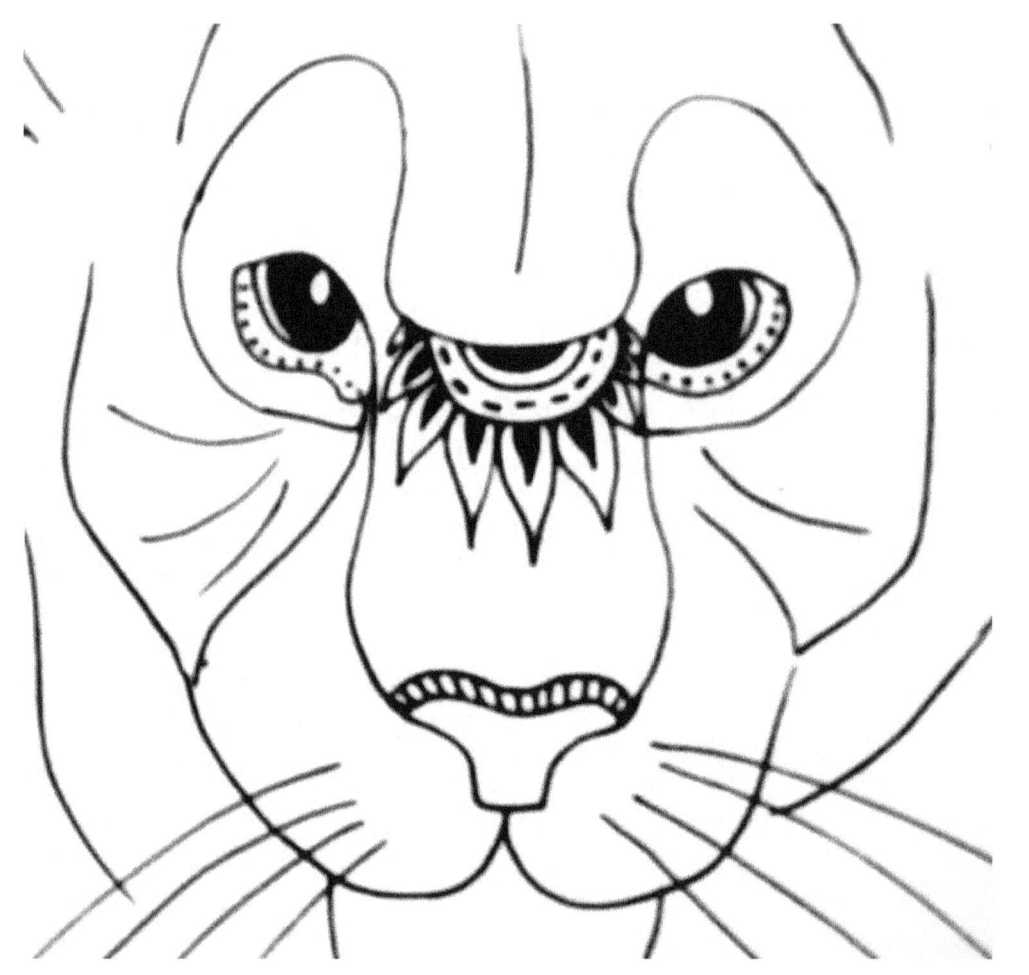

Step two: We will now concentrate on the eyes and the nose. The process will be the same for both eyes: paint black the space between the drop and the curved line, then in the space between the eye and the line below it make several dots. For the upper part of the nose, we will be working with free arcs, one inside the other, the smaller one will be painted black, and the bigger one will have sketched horizontal lines following the shape of the arcs;

Right below it, you will make the petals of these 'flower'-they will be made by the union of two curved lines each, or a curved triangle- inside of it there shall be another one equal, but smaller and filled with black. Then for the lowest part of the nose, make an "m" doubled curved shape, one parallel to the other, with some parallel diagonal lines inside.

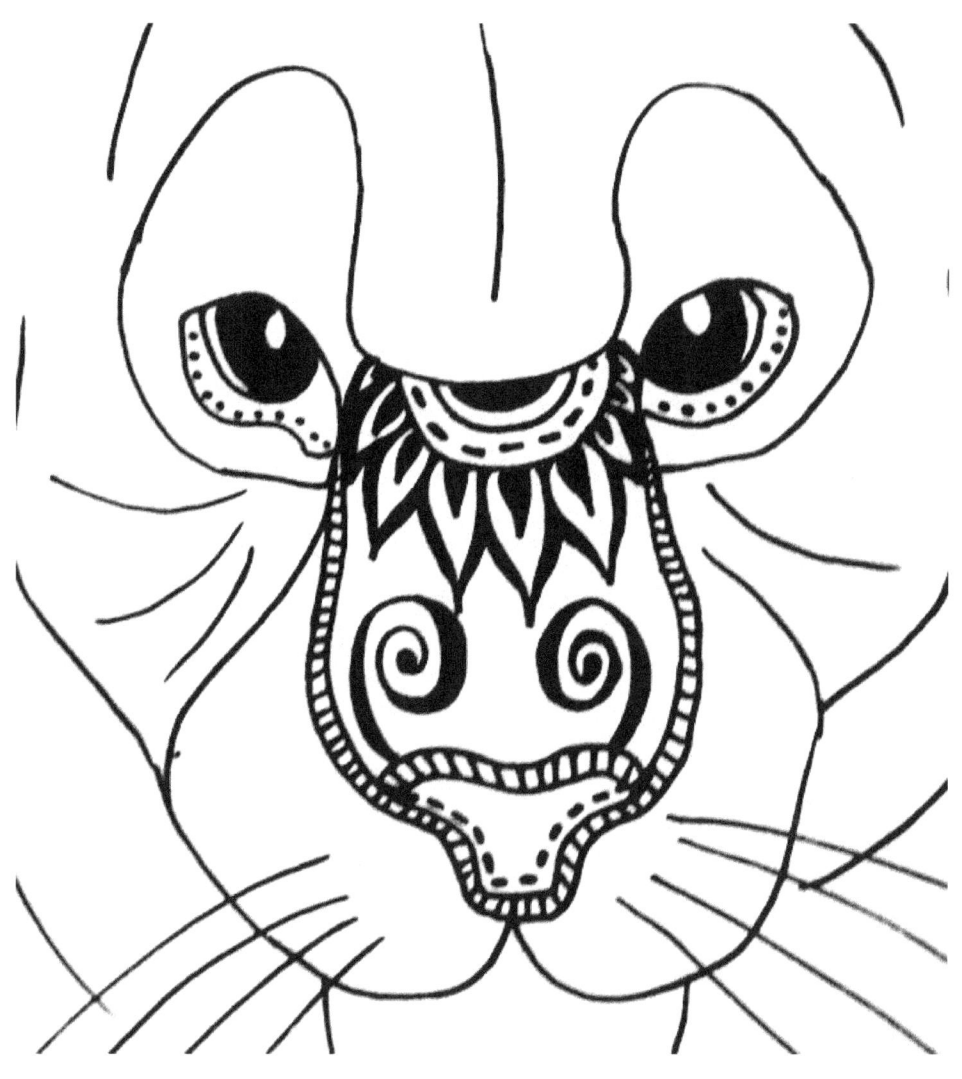

Step three: For the petals on the upper part of the nose, we will be painting a thicker outline. Then make a parallel line for both sides of the nose, make horizontal lines inside of it. Above the "m" double lined curve, make two similar spirals with thick lines.

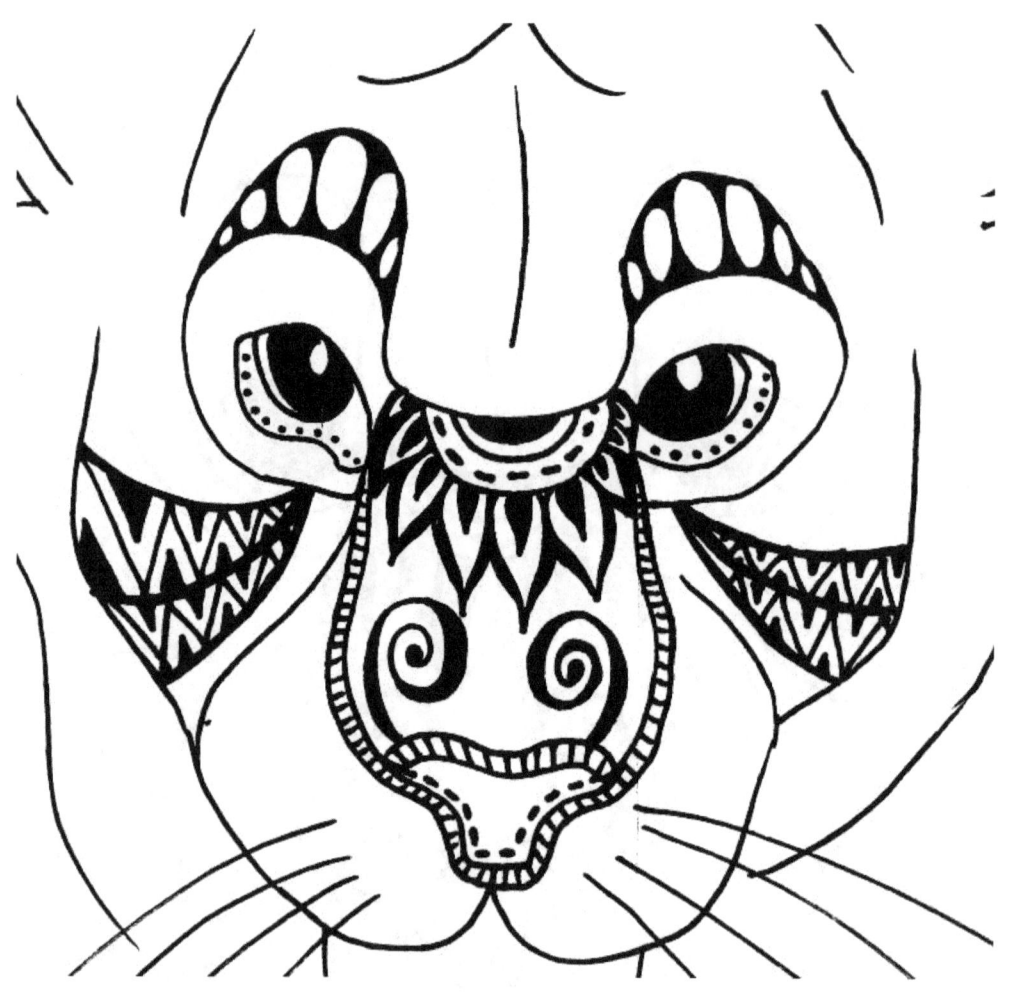

Step four: Now, and keeping with the idea of repeating the process of one side on the other, just a bit below the arc above the eye make another arched line, in the space they're created make several ovals, paint the space between them black. Create a triangular figure; filled with upside and down triangles, and with smaller ones inside them that will be black-it should look like a wellie-. This last figure will go from the sides of the face to the lower part of the eye.

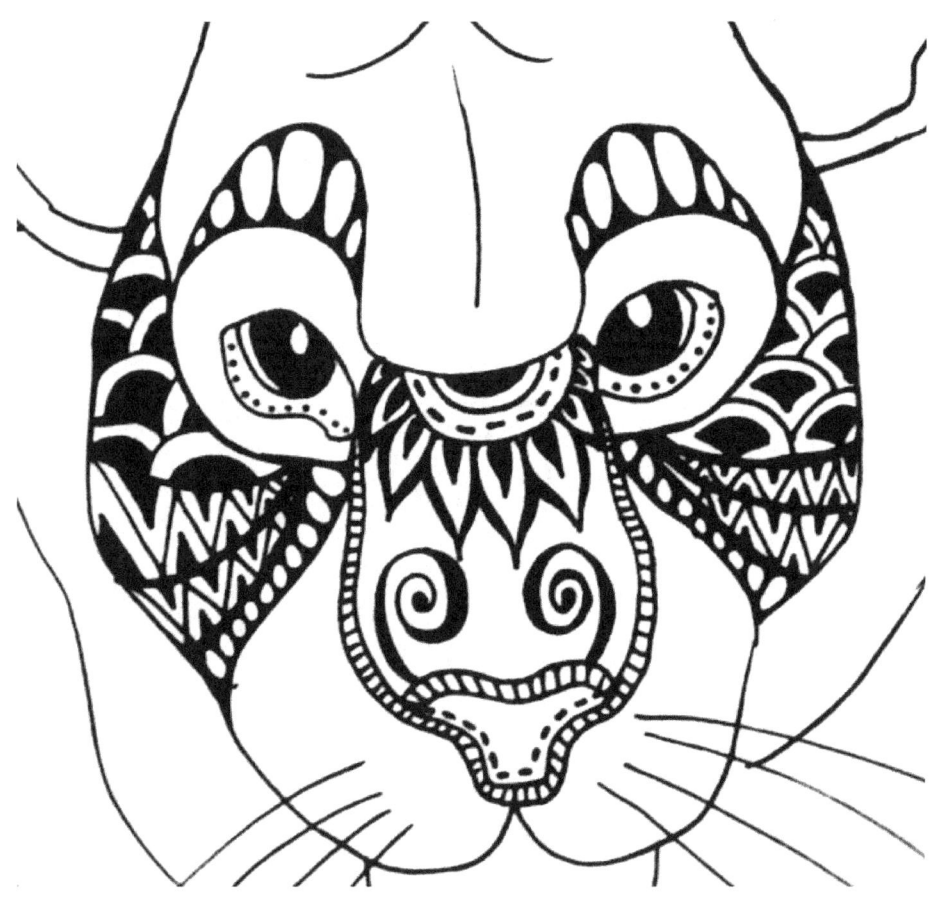

Step five: Below this triangle shaped figure make a thick line with small circles inside of it. Above mentioned figure make various semi circles with black smaller arcs inside of them.

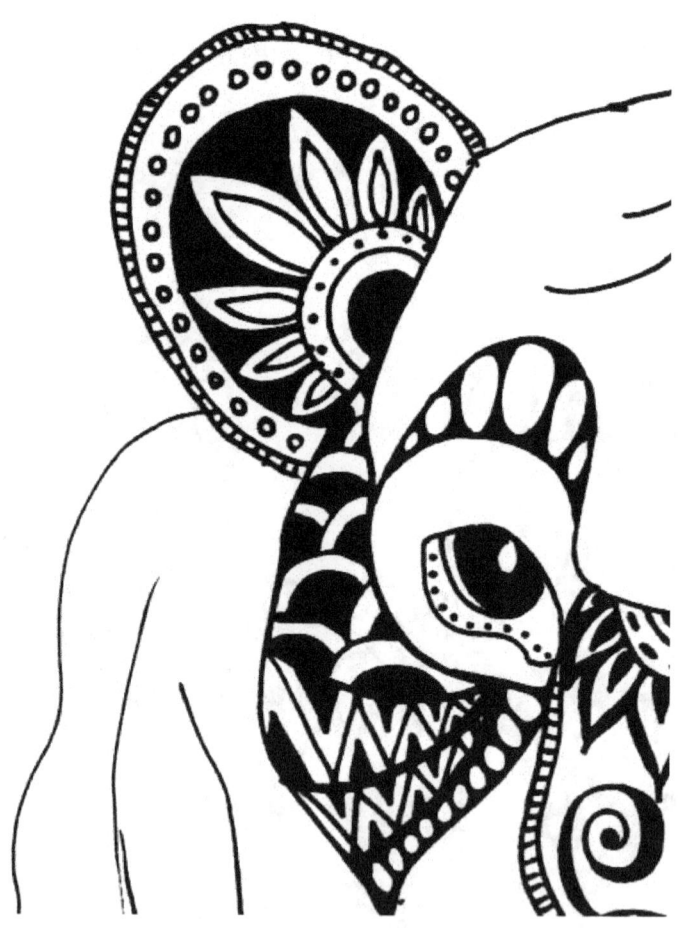

Step six: for the left ear we will be repeating the process we used to make the flower shape of the nose; the difference will be that we will be leaving the petals blank, and we will have dots instead of lines-the space surrounding the flower will be black-. Apart, a parallel line will follow the arc of the ear, and horizontal lines will be put inside the space between them; at the same time small circles will be put following the shape of the ear in the void between the black and the line.

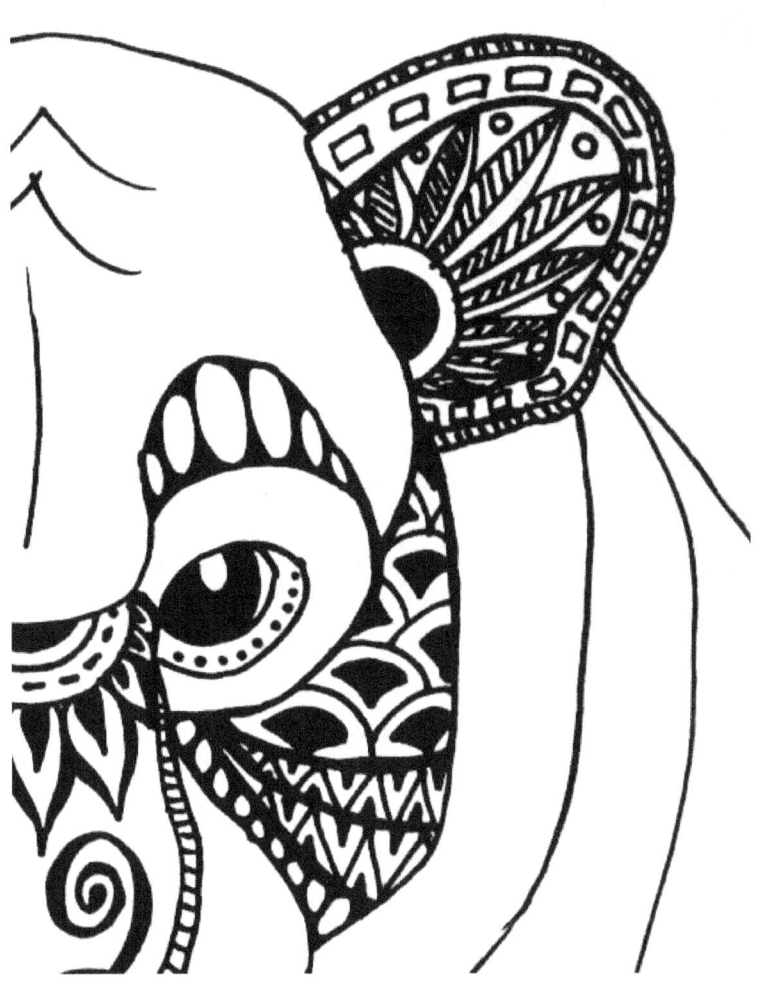

Step seven: Repeat the flower process on the right ear, but now add one vertical line to each petal, dividing it, on one side make parallel diagonal lines; for the arc inside and arc just paint the smaller one black; in the blank between petals draw circles. Repeat the process of drawing a parallel line with horizontal lines inside. Then make small rectangle shaped figures following the outline of the ear, and below this make a thick line engulfing the flower figure.

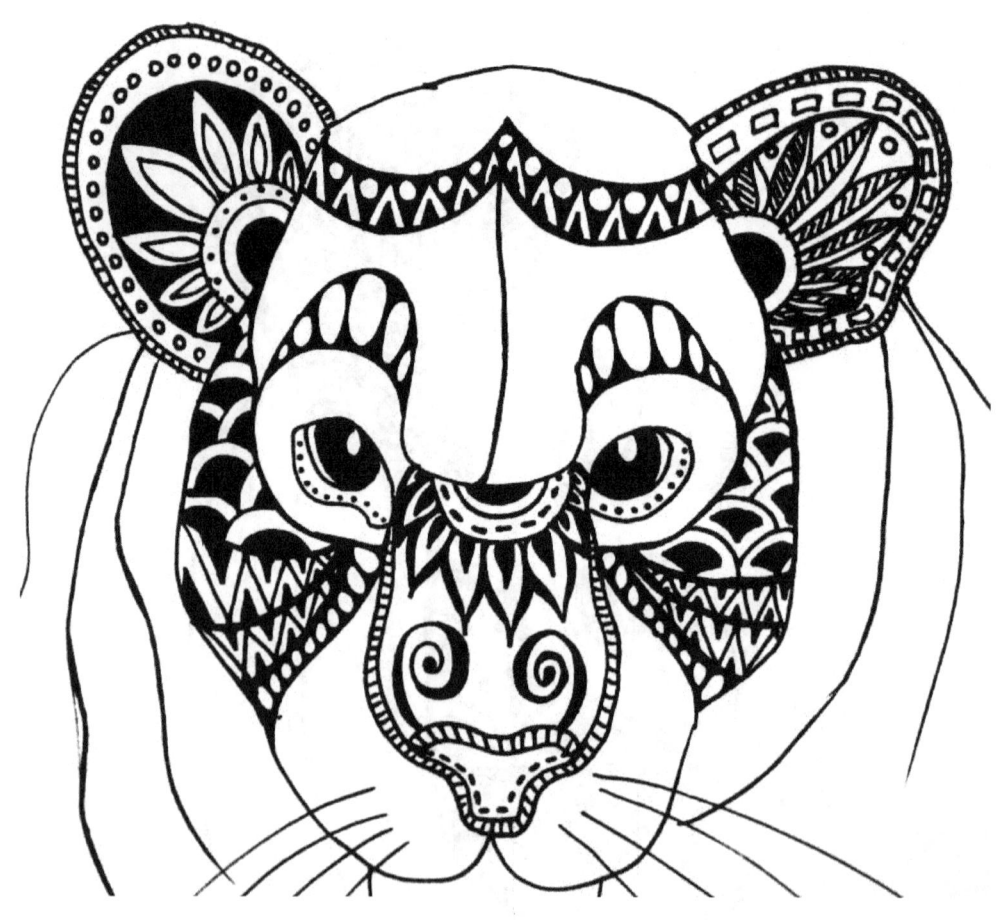

Step eight: Now the forehead of the creature will be made taking the "v" lines we talk far by on step one, making them continue both to the sides of the head and to the center. Then make upside down "v"s inside this new figure, with blank dots above. Fill the space between the parallel lines with black.

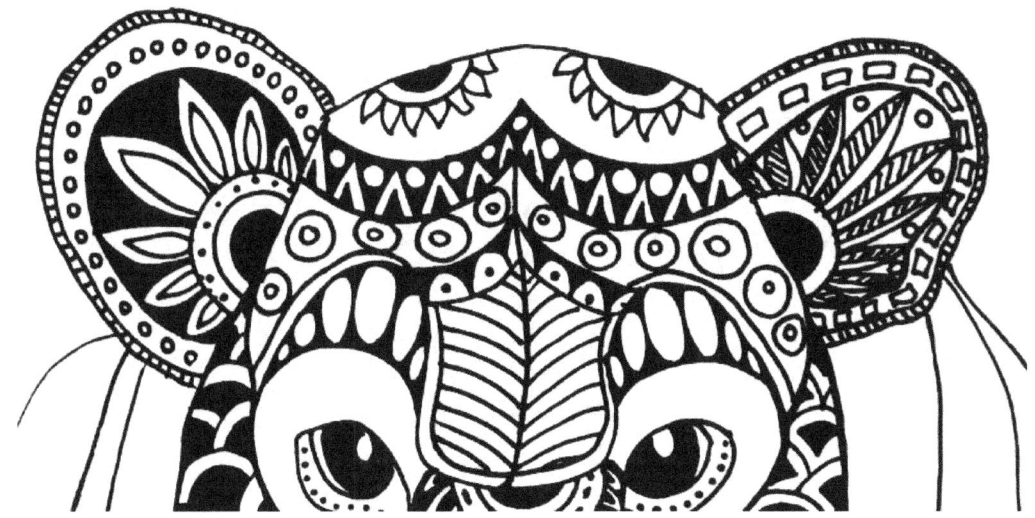

Step nine: Taking the curved vertical line between both eyes we will start making curved horizontal lines for both sides. Then make a parallel outline, leaving a space, for the limiting area of the eyes and eyebrows. With the shape of the wallies, make a second row below and fill it with circles with smaller circles inside, then in the space between the eyebrows make tiny arcs with dots inside them, leave the area around it black. On the top of the head make two figures that look like sunflowers with the inner semicircle being black.

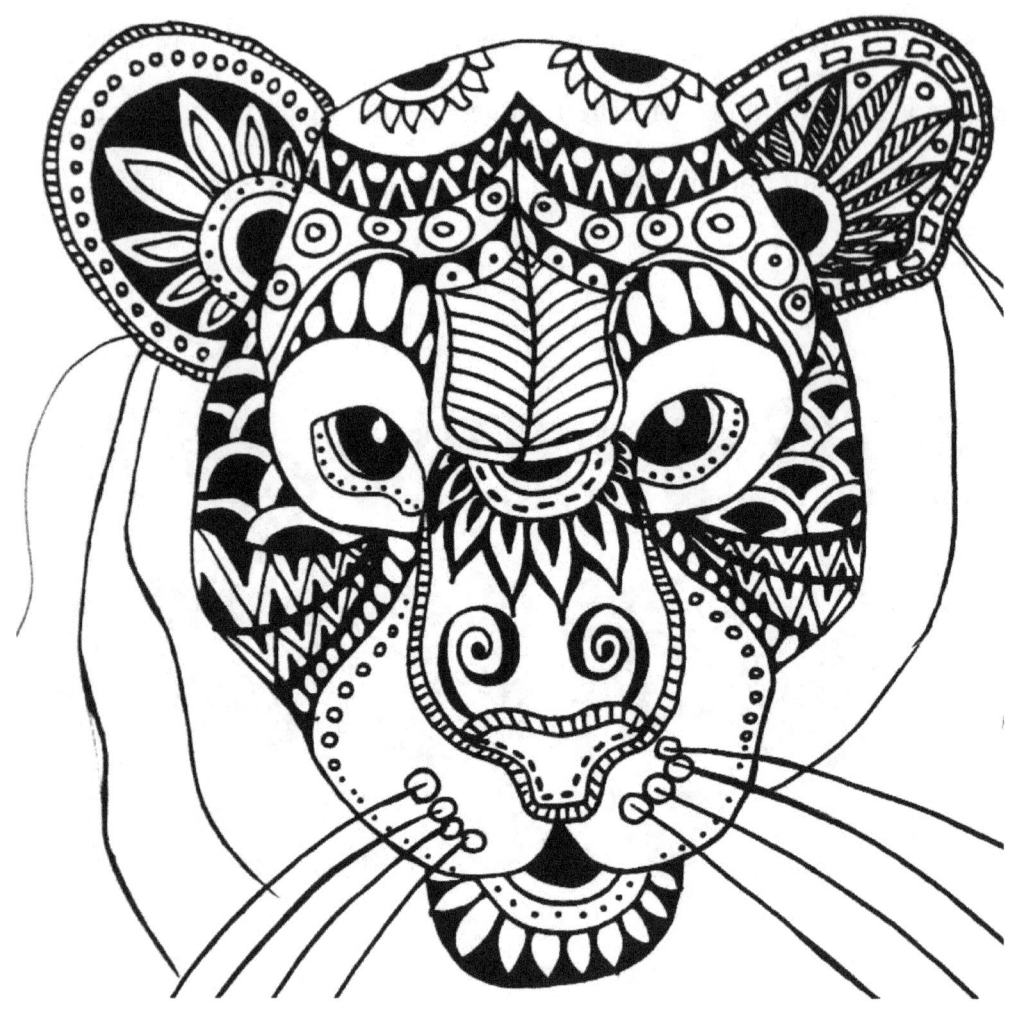

Step ten: Moving on to the upper part of the mouth, draw various blank dots that will follow the outline of it; use circles for the starting point of the whiskers. To make the gape of the mouth fill the space between the upper and lower part with black. On the lower part of the mouth make four semicircles, on the bigger one make small dots following the same shape. After this, draw petals for this 'flower', then make the surrounding area black.

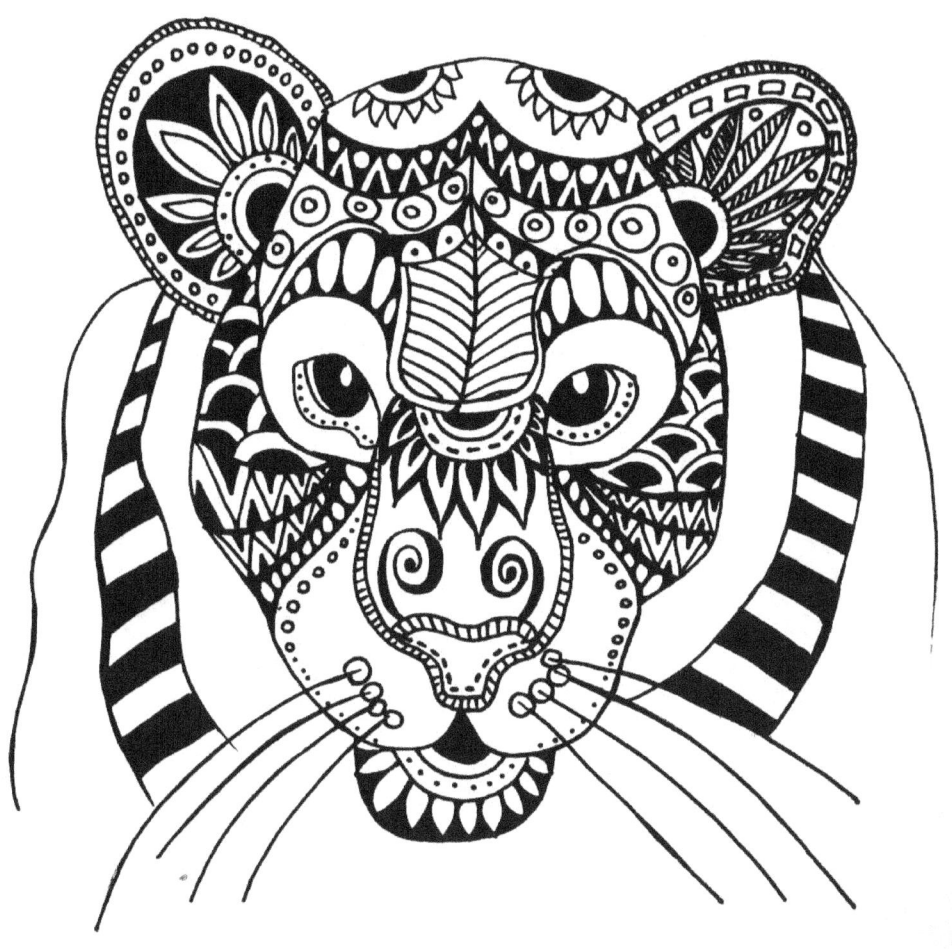

Step eleven: On the sides of the face, make a parallel line for that already drawn, and in the space in between make various horizontal lines with some space between them, in every other space fill it with black.

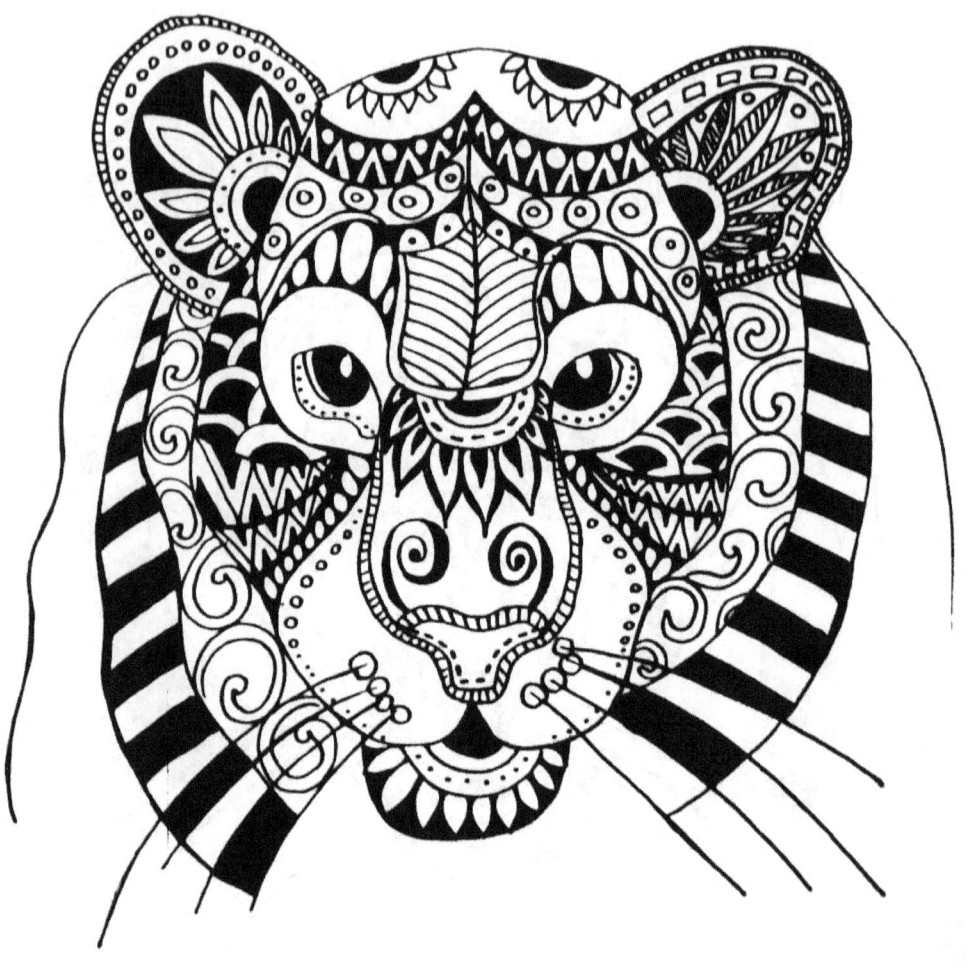

Step twelve: On the space between the prior step and the face make various curved lines and spirals with double lines and blank in the middle.

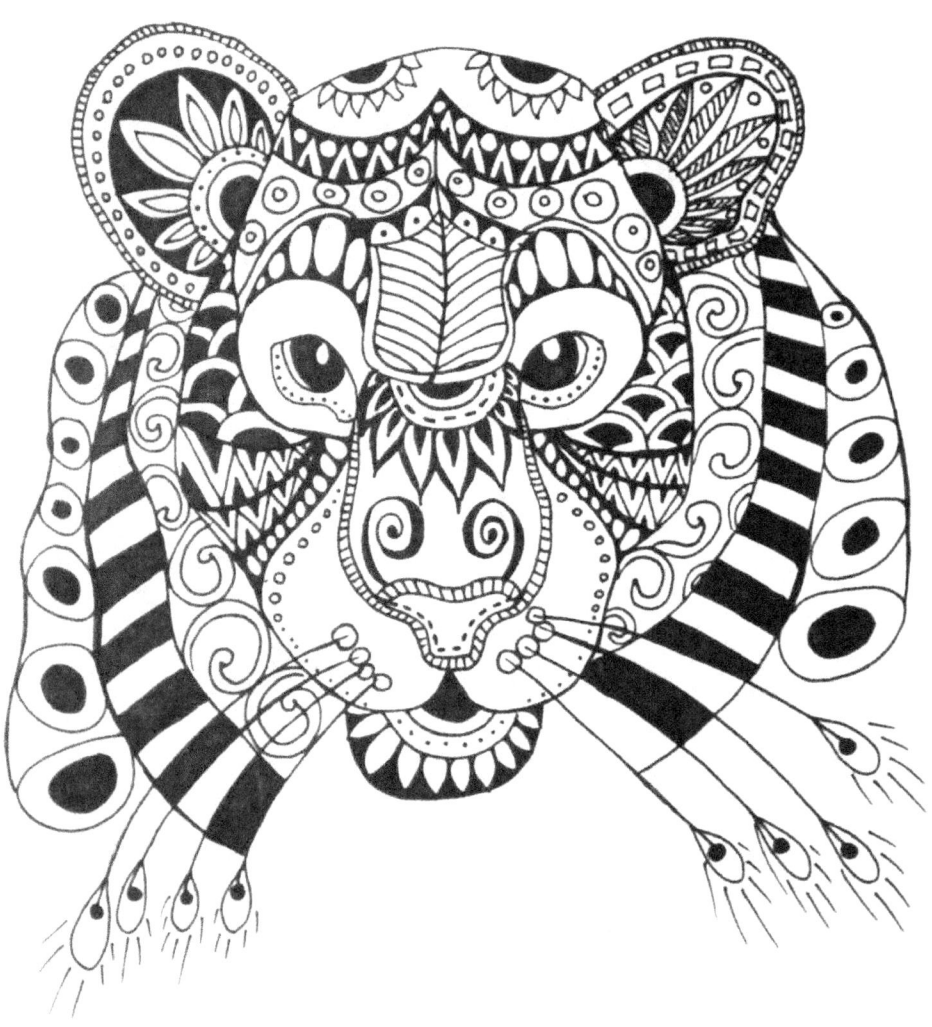

Step thirteen: For the part nearest the outline draw various circles with a smaller black circles inside of each. On the point of the whiskers make drops with thick dots and with sketched lines.

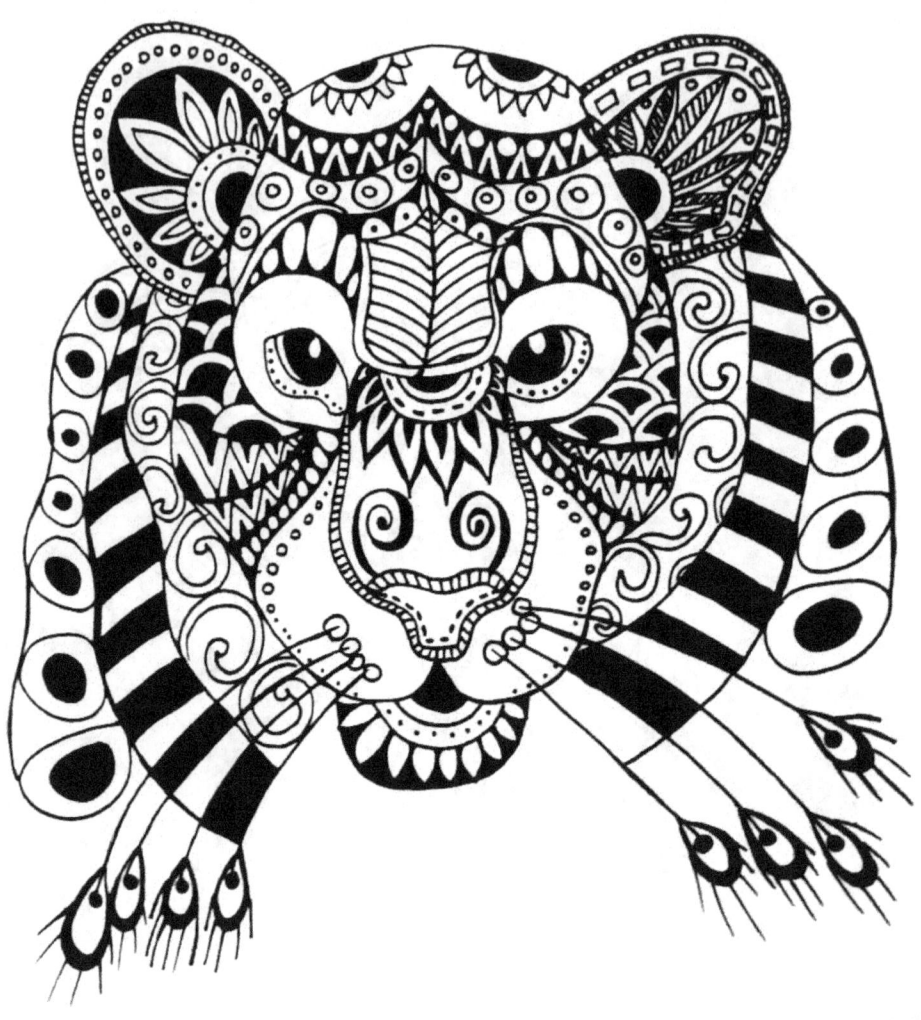

Step fourteen: Inside the drops make a thicker line following the outline.

Our tiger is ready!

Drawing level 6: A majestic peacock

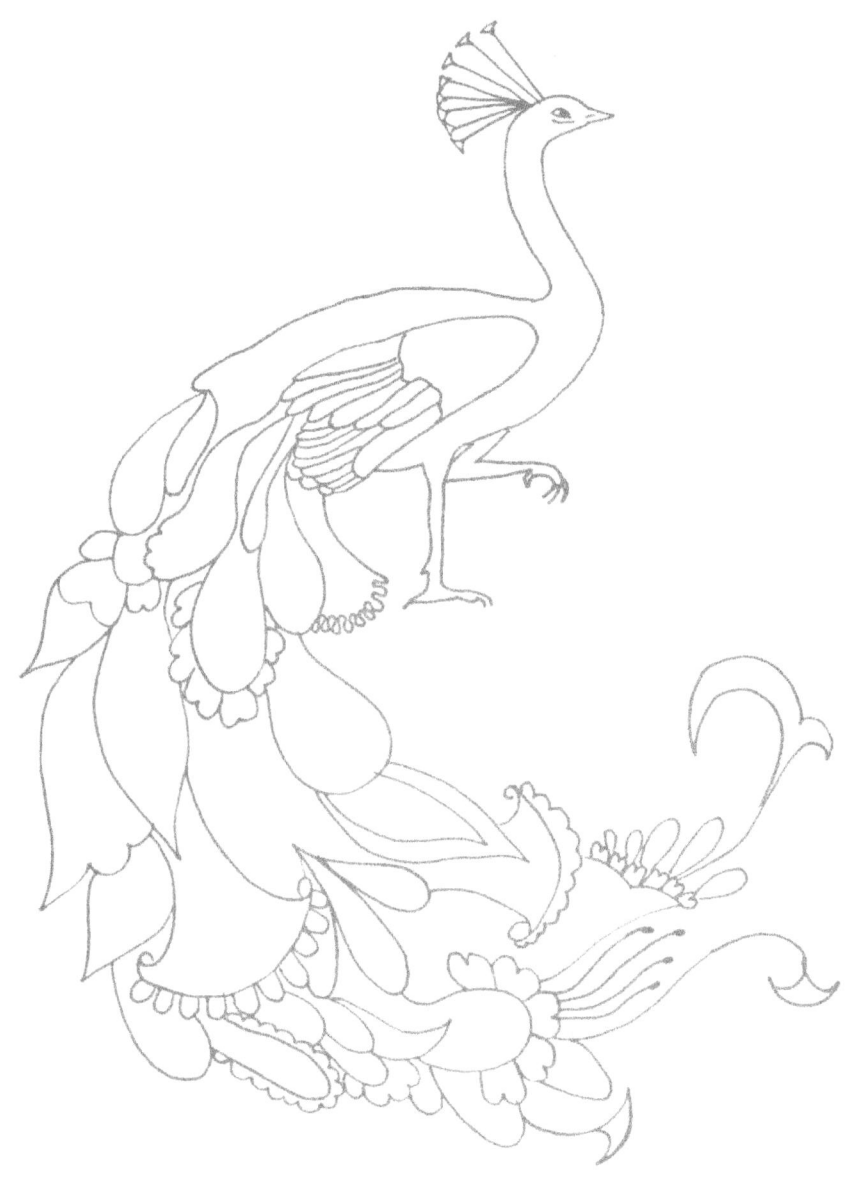

Step one: The base for these creature will be a 'two' for the upper part and a's' for the lower part; for the upper part we will have a beak and one oval with a small black dot inside. On the top of the head make various straight lines with triangles on the upper part. Then for the legs and claws use sketched lines for the legs, and curved ones for the claws.

For the side plumage use long drop like shapes one on top of the other, in a diagonal inclination, leaving a bell like shape on the part nearest to the body, with the plumage descending towards the tail. For the feathers of the tail use big drop like figures and base like figures, on the bottom of each feather use various arcs to ornament. Also make some curved lines for the last part of the tail; and with some motifs at their points, some even with dots.

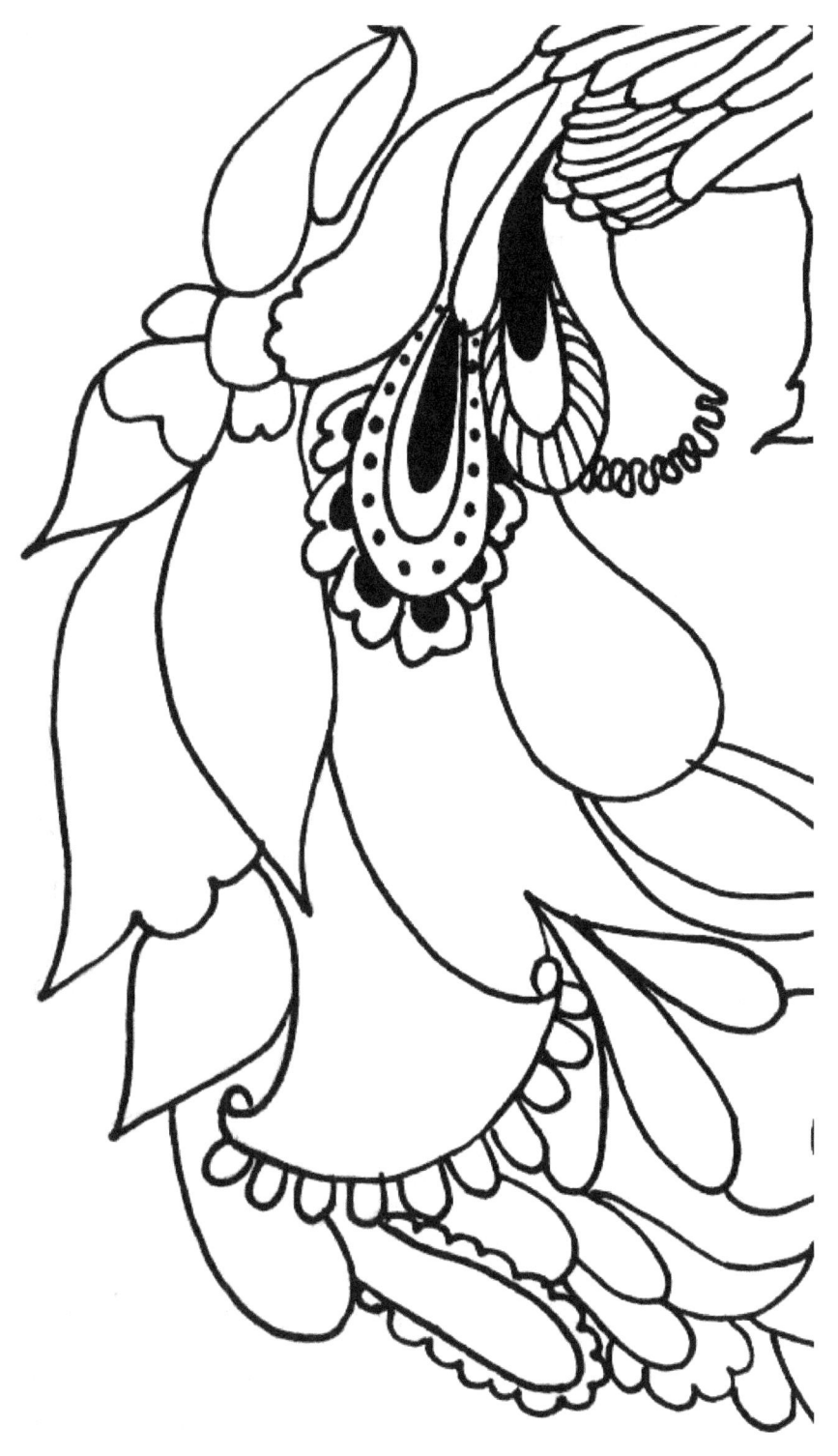

Step two: We will start working with two feathers; on both we will put one smaller inside painted black; surrounded it - two other similar outlines-still inside of each primary drop like feather-. For one figure you will draw vertical lines in the space between the second to last and the outline; and for the other one, on the same place make various dots. Continuing on this one, draw black semicircles on the ornaments of the feather.

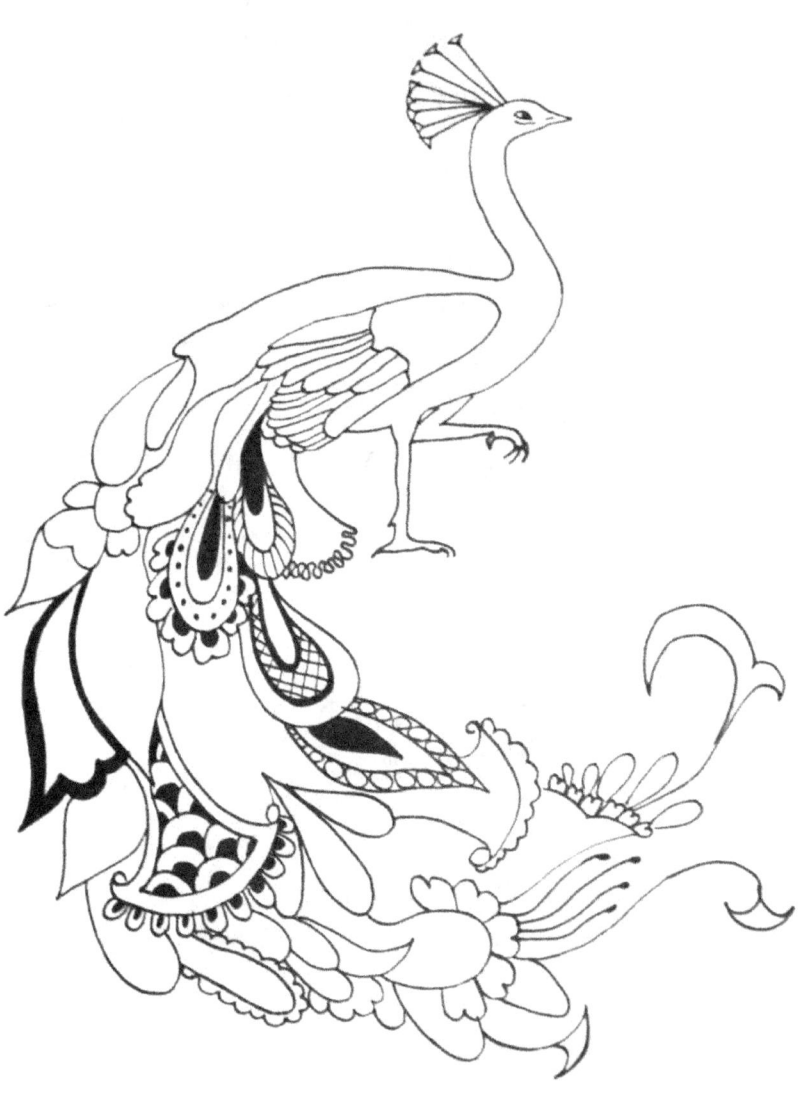

Step three: Next we will continue working with motifs for various feathers. First we will take one feather, make two drops inside of it, one inside of the other. Put the outline of them being thicker and create a net of lines in the space between them. Moving to the side of the bird chose one of the bigger feathers and put outline with a very thick line.

Then move to another plumage that looks more like a base, fill it with arcs, with small black semicircles inside, leaving a surrounding white area. Then for the ornament do the same work you d
id for the arcs and semicircles.

Another feather will have the outline shape repeated inside one inside the other, leaving some space between them. Put circles inside them; paint the smaller figure with black.

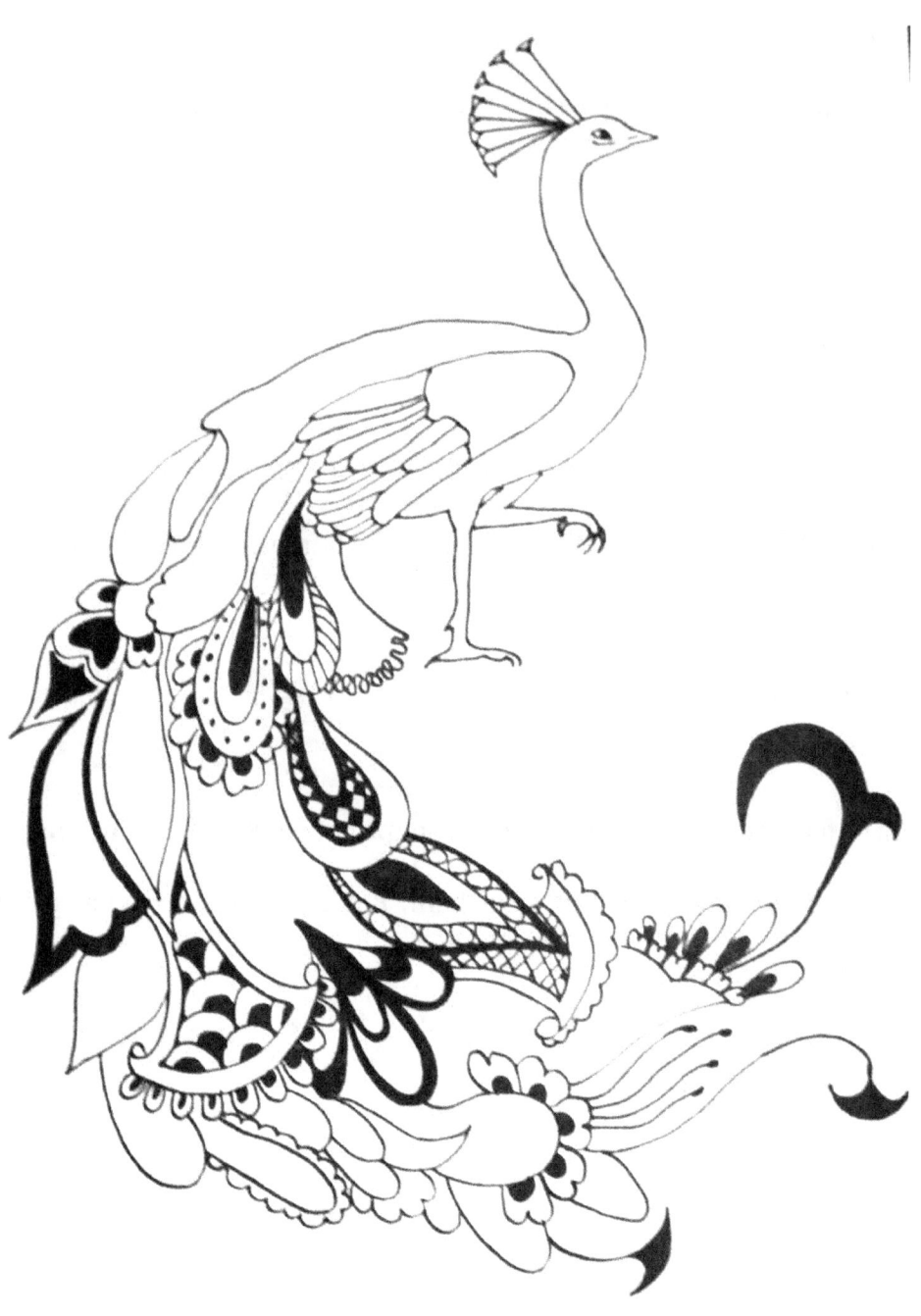

Step four: Continuing with the last feather we tackle we will make a thicker line. For the base like figure behind it, draw an equal in shape but smaller one with webs inside it. For the net made one step prior paint some of the squares formed with black. Take the smaller feather and create a copy in them that will be black. For the curves coming from the tail, paint the motifs on top of them black too.

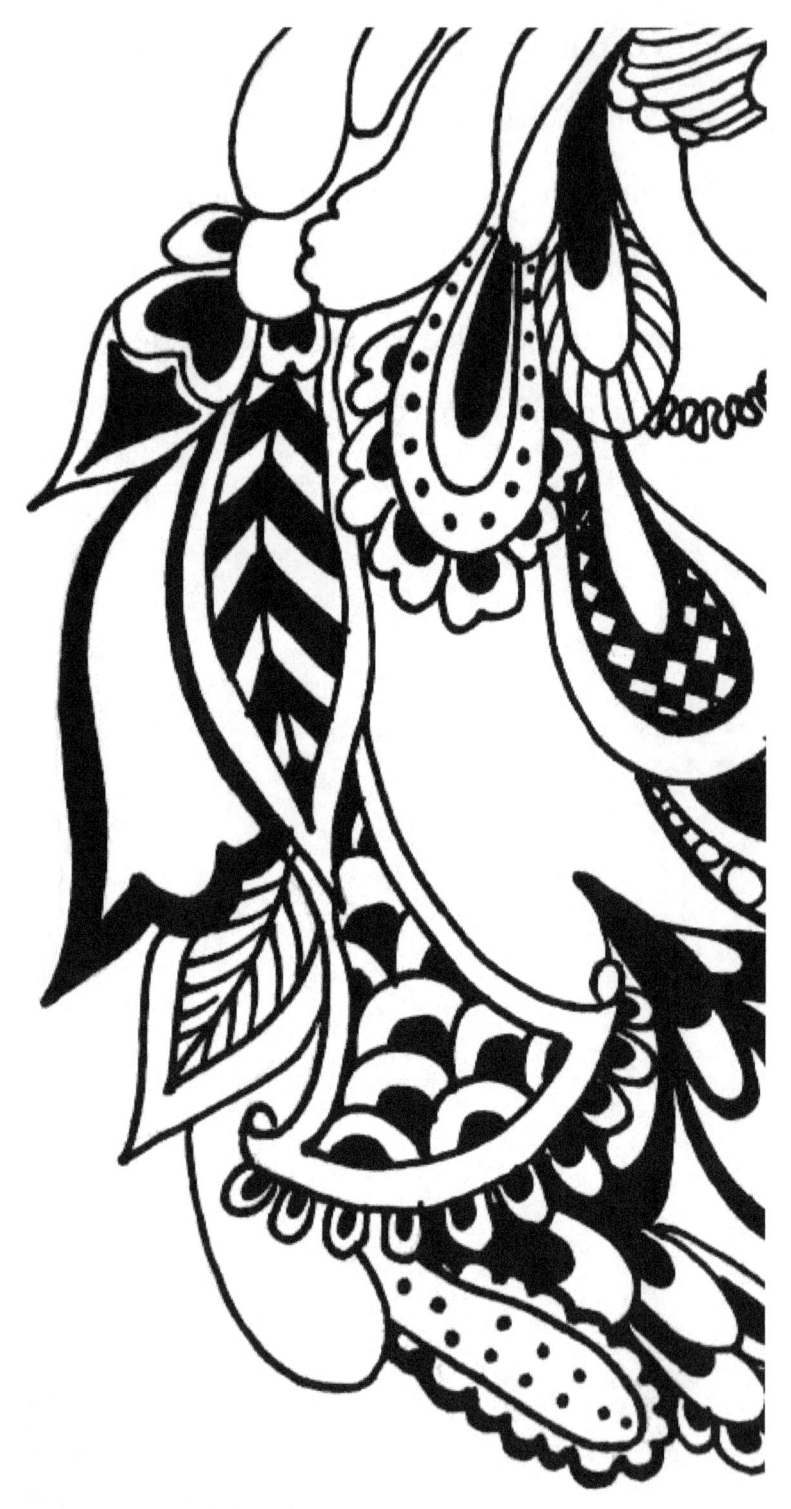

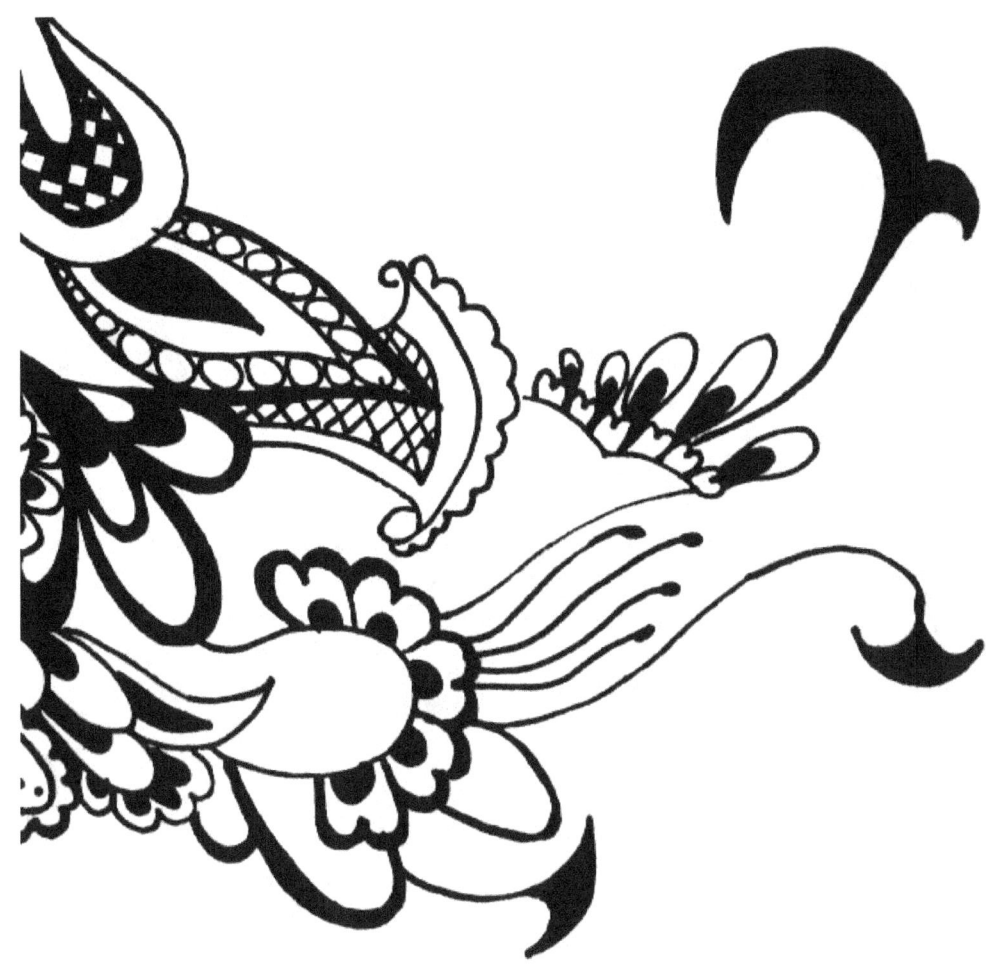

Step five: Now we will take one of the feathers, nearest the bottom. We will make one figure smaller inside of the other; this smaller one will be divided by a curved line; inside of these we will have diagonal lines going on different directions. Then make smaller dots inside another feather, outline it with thicker lines. Make smaller black figures following the outlines of various smaller feathers, painting the inside of these ones black.

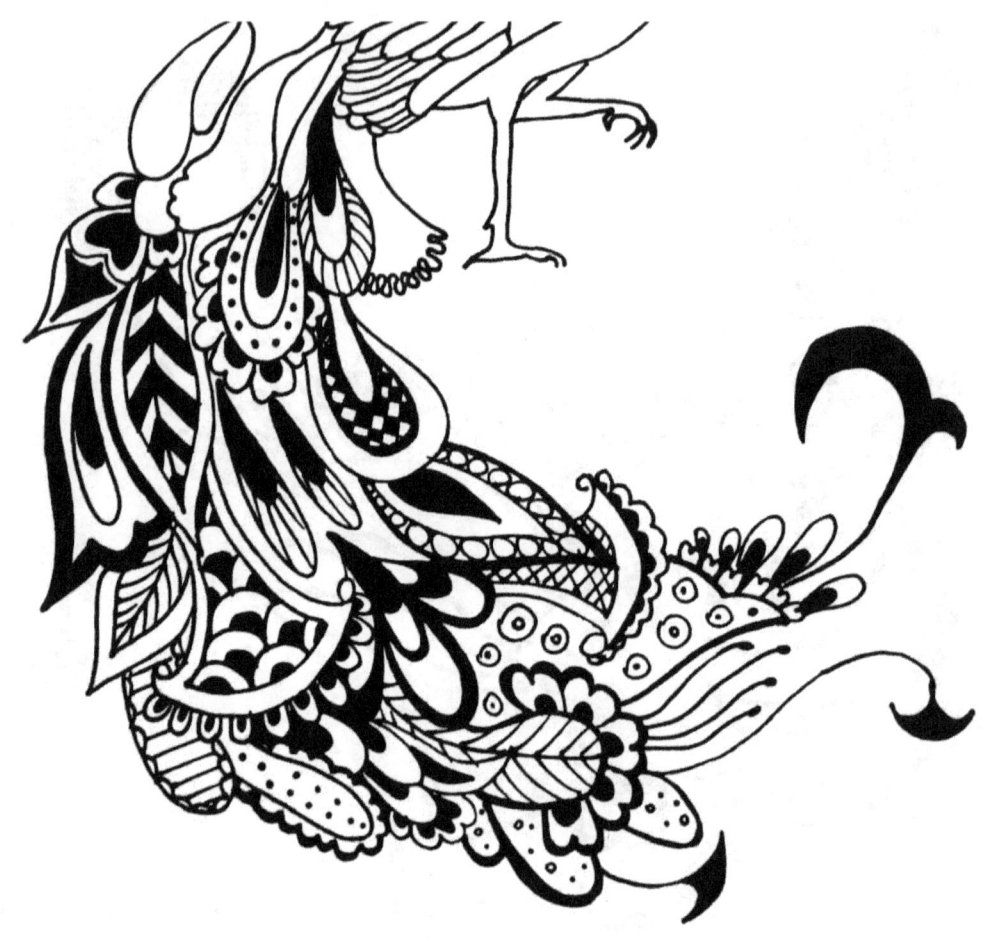

Step six: We will put horizontal lines inside one of the feathers, with the inside surrounding area being completed with small arcs. Inside the other feathers put some dots and small circles.

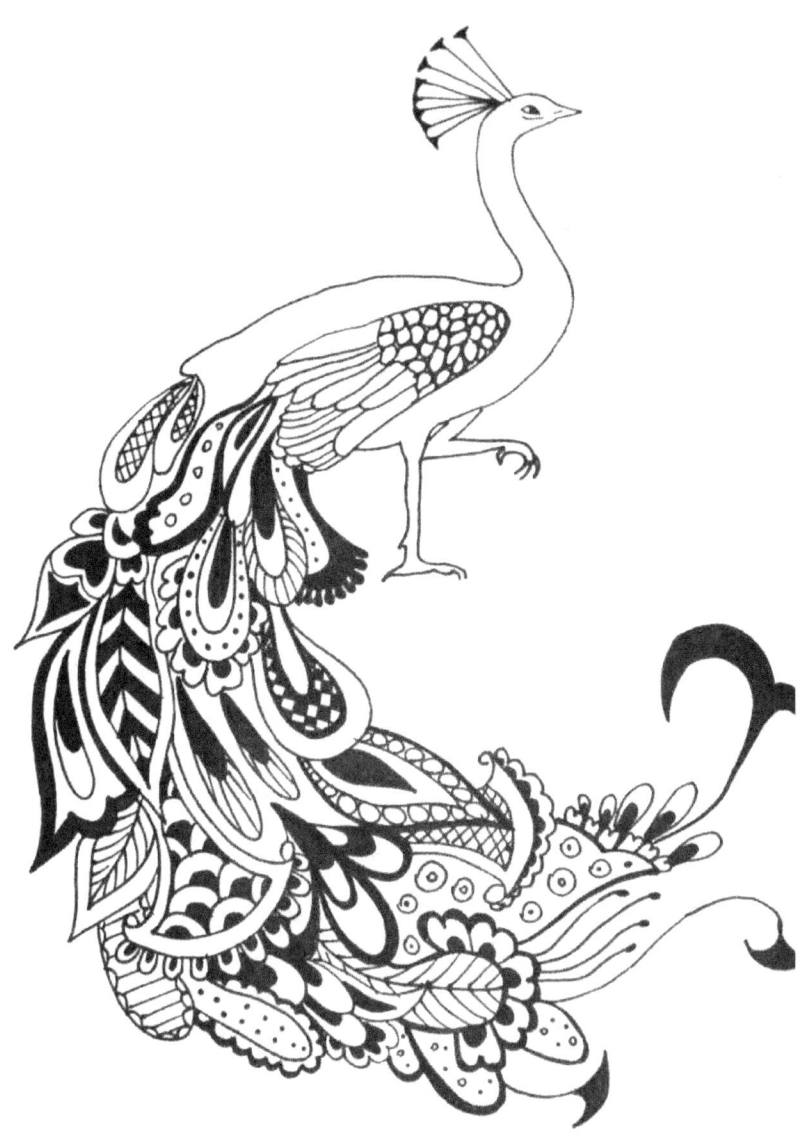

Step seven: For the plumage on the body, or rather the feathers, draw inside the larger area stone like irregular shapes. Move to the tail and make some nets inside some of the feathers, and make thick outlines for others.

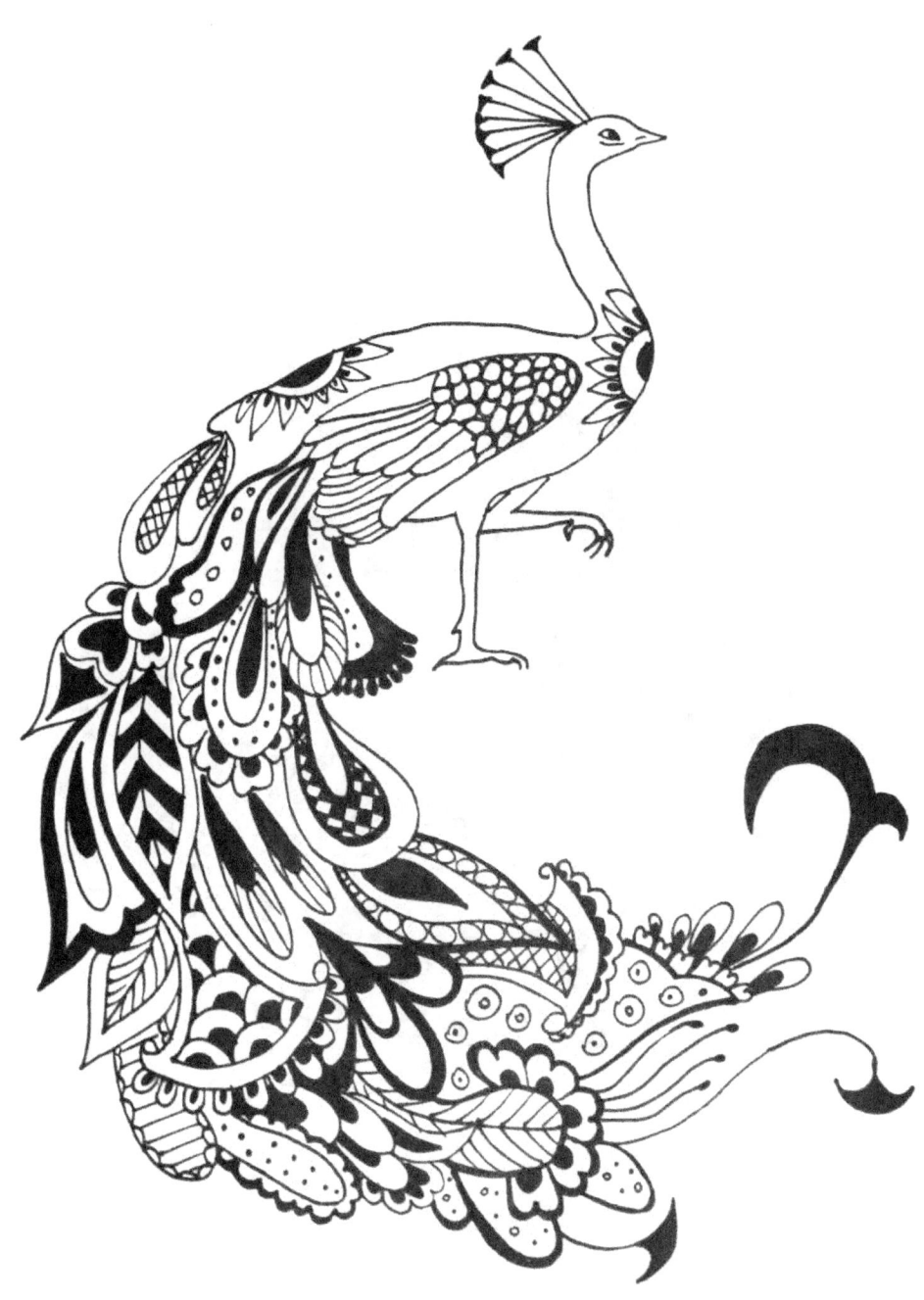

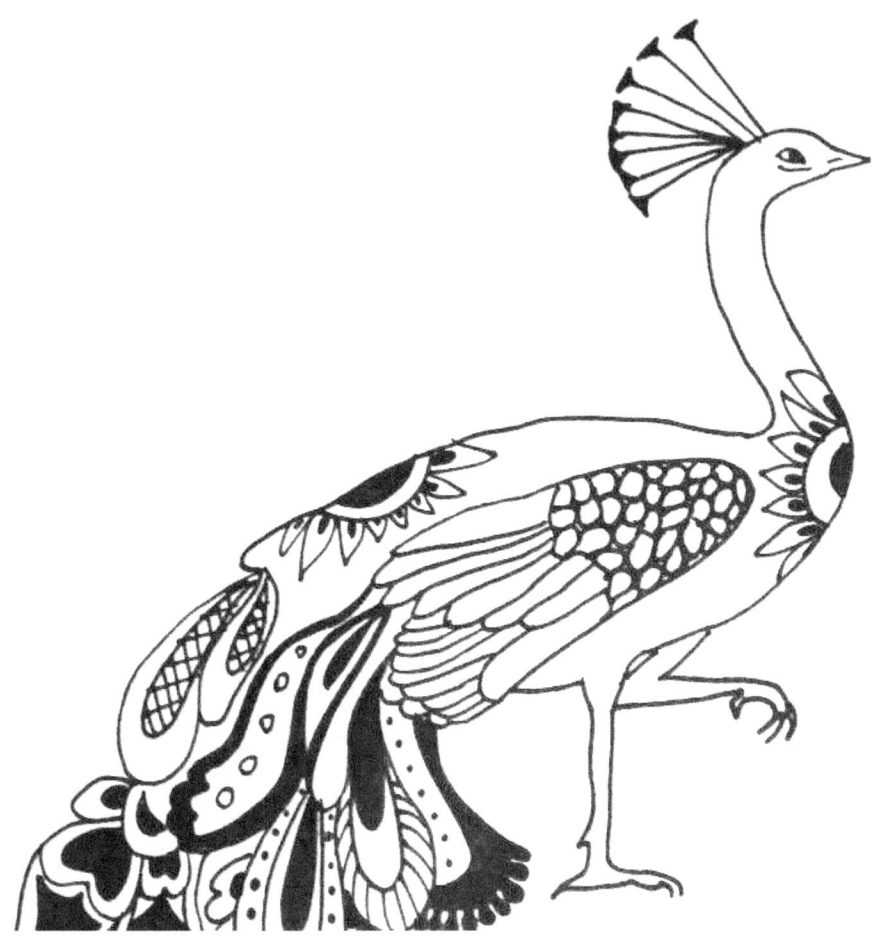

Step eight: Finally, make two sunflowers like figures, one on the chest and the other on the back. They will have a smaller circle inside a bigger one and smaller petal inside the bigger one; all of these smaller figures will be painted black. And there you will have your peacock. You can play with the motifs and making lines thinner or thicker as you wish.

Conclusion

Now we have just got to the end of the book; all of these lessons are supposed to help you to get a hold of this art form. We suppose that you have notice how an animal and vegetable motives are repeated over and over here; another figure that is frequently used is that of spirals and curves.

This sort of sketches is recommended to be drawn with markers, because we are not supposed to erase or correct while working with this type of style. More exactly, this is not working at all, this is something that should be use for recreation, so making mistakes is not a thing that you or anyone else should care about; this is about relaxing.

ZEN doodles is not only a drawing technique, it is also based around the goal of letting your inner artist run free with any crazy idea, so you can express it on the paper; also doubles as some sort of meditation technique.

The drawings do not even need to be as complicated as the ones already shown, it can be just circles and spirals, flakes and drops, peacock feathers and shields, and it all depends on your imagination. So get a piece of paper, a marker, and draw something.

Thank you!

Thank you for choosing our book, we hope you found it interesting and helpful.

If you liked the book, please give us a favor to write your review here:

We would really appreciate this!

If you would like to have a bonus – **FREE BOOK**, please send the screenshot of your review to this e-mail:

lucy.artbooks@gmail.com and we will send you a **FREE BOOK** in PDF as a **GIFT!****

Hope to see you in our future books and good luck in your drawing experience!

** in the e-mail subject please mention the name of the book you reviewed and the author.

Other books from Daniele Ling

Drawing People in Zen Doodle Technique: Unleash Your Creativity with Unique Zen Doodle People Drawing

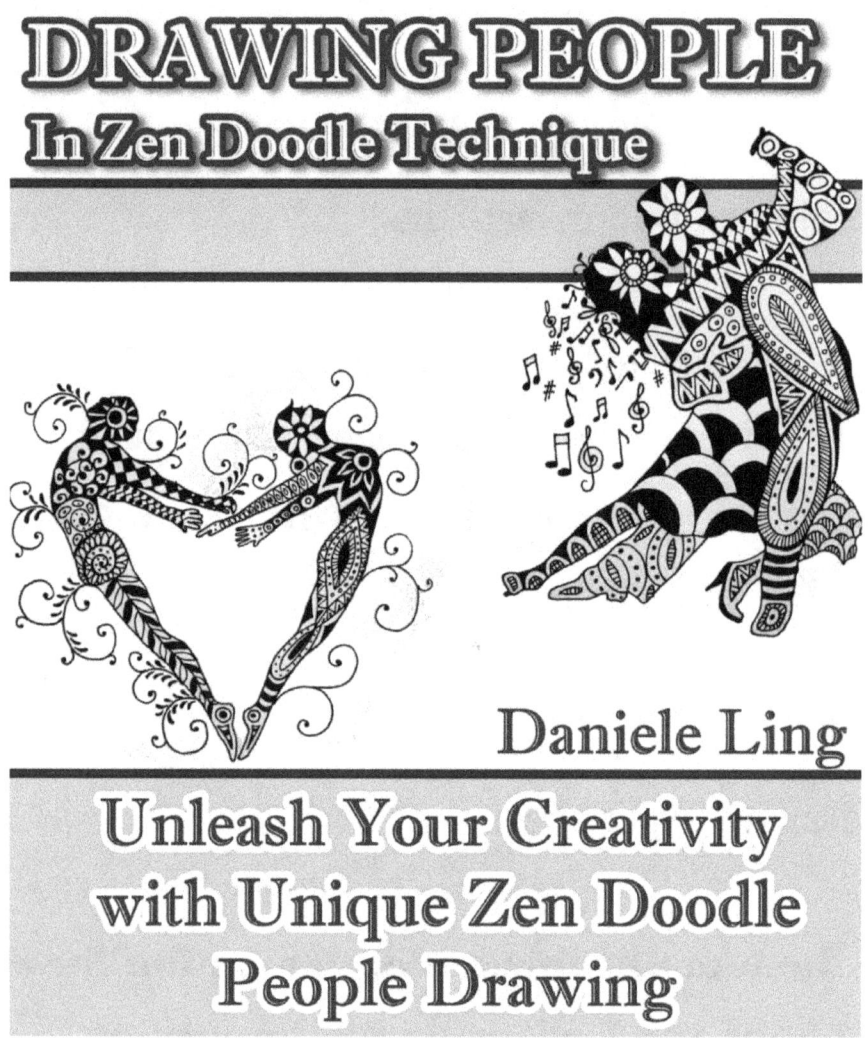

Zen Doodle Cats:

Drawing Zen Doodle Cats Made Easy

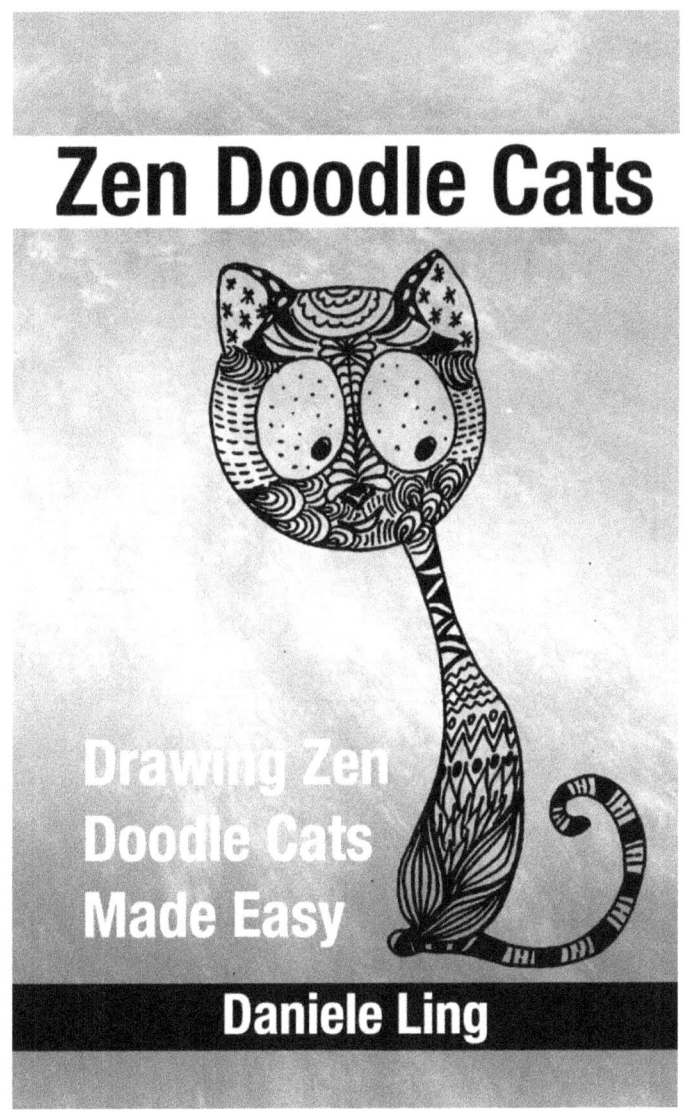

Zen Doodle Imagination: Create Your Own Zen Doodle Drawings Easy!

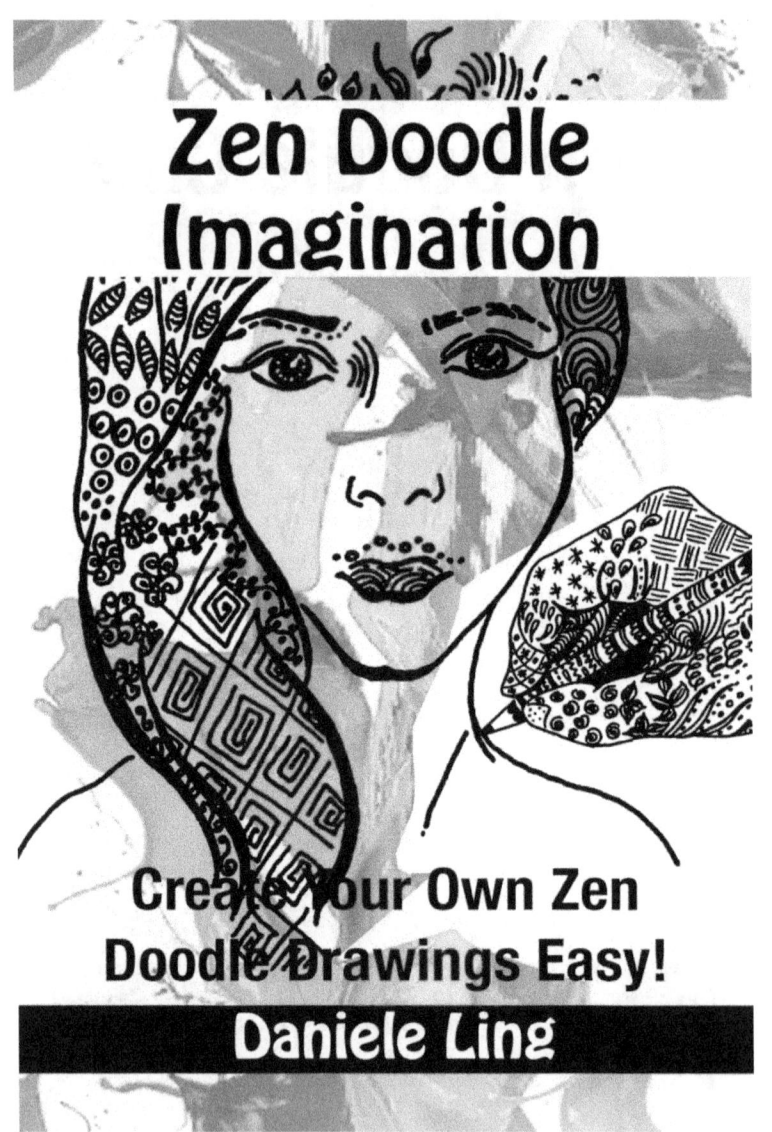

Zen Dogs Drawing: Learn how to Draw Your Favorite Dogs with Zen Doodle!

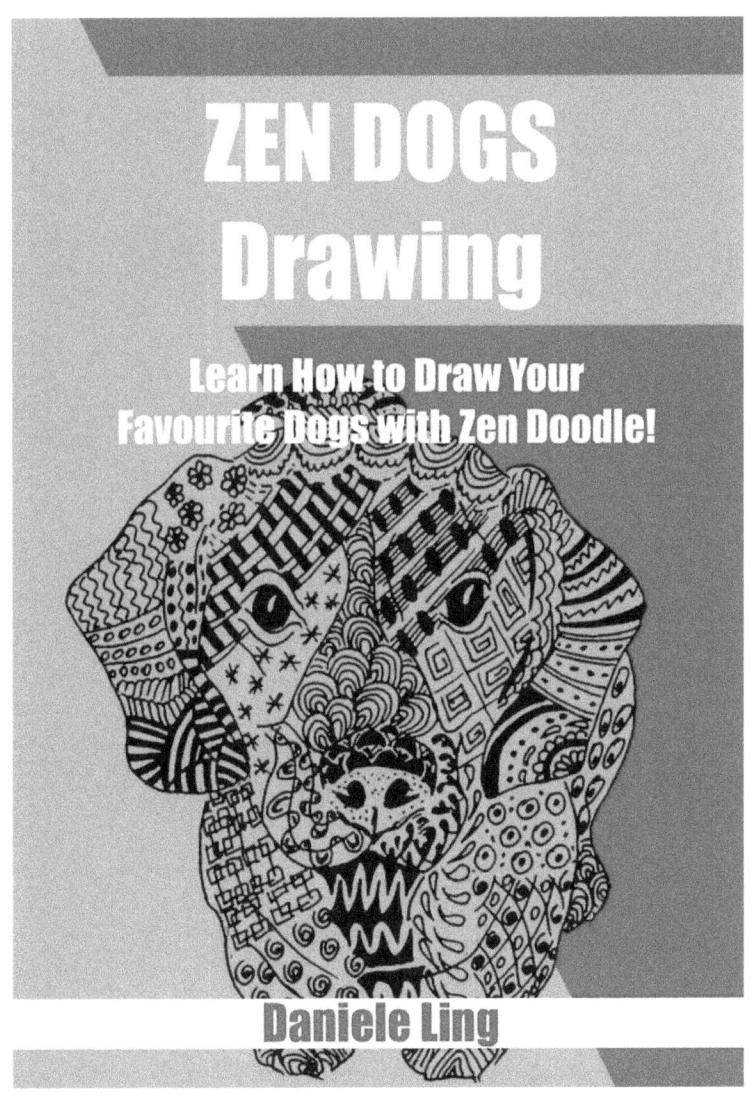

www.ingramcontent.com/pod-product-compliance
Lightning Source LLC
Chambersburg PA
CBHW080705190526
45169CB00006B/2251